Demystifying Disney

Demystifying Disney
A History of Disney Feature Animation

Chris Pallant

continuum

2011

The Continuum International Publishing Group
80 Maiden Lane, New York, NY 10038
The Tower Building, 11 York Road, London SE1 7NX

www.continuumbooks.com

Pallant, C. Material included in Chapter Three previously published in part, by SAGE Publications (Los Angeles, London, New Delhi, Singapore, Washington DC) in 'Disney-Formalism: Rethinking "Classic Disney"'. *Animation: An Interdisciplinary Journal* 5(3): 341–352.

Pallant, C. Material featured in Chapter Seven previously published in part, by Intellect Journals in 'Neo-Disney: Recent developments in Disney feature animation'. *New Cinemas: Journal of Contemporary Film* 8(2): 103–117.

Library of Congress Cataloging-in-Publication Data
    Pallant, Chris.
    Demystifying Disney : a history of animation/by Chris Pallant.
       p. cm.
    Section 1: Re-examining Disney – Disney authorship – A history of innovation – Section 2: Early and middle Disney feature animation –Disney formalism – Destino – Disney in transition – Section 3: Contemporary Disney feature animation – The Disney renaissance – Neo-Disney – Digital Disney – Conclusion: 'Happily ever after'.
    Includes bibliographical references and index.
    ISBN-13: 978-1-4411-7421-5 (hardcover: alk. paper)
    ISBN-10: 1-4411-7421-4 (hardcover: alk. paper) 1. Animated films–United States–History and criticism. 2. Walt Disney Company. I. Title.

NC1766.U52D5543 2011
741.5'8–dc22

                                                                        2010044419

ISBN: HB: 978-1-4411-7421-5

Typeset by Newgen Imaging Systems Pvt Ltd, chennai, India.
Printed and bound in the United States of America

Contents

Acknowledgements

A number of people have contributed to the creation of this book and deserve special mention. This book first came into being as a PhD thesis, therefore profound thanks are due to my supervisor, Steven Price, who helped shape the text in its original form. Additionally, the advice offered by Paul Wells, who examined the thesis, proved useful when adapting the text for publication. I would also like to express sincere gratitude to the many individuals working at the British Library, in the special collections department at the British Film Institute and in the Fales Archive at the Bobst Library in New York, for their tireless professionalism during my archival visits. At Continuum, the enthusiasm and expertise of David Barker and Katie Gallof warrant special praise; without their efforts this book would not exist. And lastly, thanks go to the men and women who crafted the animation upon which this study is based.

Introduction

Tangled (2010) was a landmark film, becoming the fiftieth animated feature film to be theatrically released by Disney. No other studio can match this record of consistent feature animation production. Furthermore, few bodies of film have such universal appeal; it is almost certain that readers of this book will have a favourite Disney animated feature. Yet, beyond this level of engagement, how accurate and detailed are popular conceptions of Disney – be that the man, the studio, or the animation?[1] This book seeks to remedy such uncertainty by providing a discriminating, and at times revisionist, perspective on Disney's feature animation. But first, it is important to identify the conditions that have hindered the average viewer from developing a more discerning understanding of Disney.

Walt Disney once stated: 'I only hope that we never lose sight of one thing – that it was all started by a mouse' (Smith and Clark 2002, 1). However, before *Mickey Mouse* (1928–99) there was *Oswald the Lucky Rabbit* (1927–43), and although Oswald the Rabbit may not enjoy the worldwide fame that Mickey Mouse now does, his significance in Disney's formative development should not be overlooked. After Disney's *Alice Comedies* (1923–27), an early live-action/animation series, began to falter, he started to develop the Oswald character. In 1927, with the encouragement of his financial backers and distributors (Charles Mintz and Universal Pictures), Disney produced the first of his *Oswald the Lucky Rabbit* shorts, *Trolley Troubles* (1927). To the delight of everyone involved, the cartoons 'quickly gathered a popular audience and even began to attract the attention of animators in New York' (Watts 1997, 29). In addition to providing a 'steady flow of profits' that helped solidify 'the studio's financial situation', Oswald broke new ground, becoming 'the first Disney character to generate merchandise' (Smith 2006, 515).

Then, in 1928, 'just as everything seemed to be going so well, came one of the most devastating episodes in Walt Disney's life, an episode

---

[1] From this point forth, to reduce the inelegant repetition of Disney when used in a possessive context to denote the Disney studio, Studio – with a capitalized 'S' – will be used as a substitute when necessary.

that would haunt him throughout his career' (Gabler 2006, 106). Mintz, after seeing the fledgling Studio develop in size with a host of animator appointments, began to question how important Disney was to the production of *Oswald the Lucky Rabbit*, wondering whether he could stage a potential coup. After quietly signing many of Disney's staff members, Mintz gave Disney an ultimatum: 'come with me and be paid a generous salary, or lose everything' (Watts 1997, 29). Unfortunately for Disney, 'under the terms of his contract Oswald was the sole property of Universal Pictures and [he] had no rights in the character his studio had created' (Holliss and Sibley 1988, 14). After a difficult confrontation with Mintz, Disney stated to his wife Lillian: 'Never again . . . will I work for somebody else' (Holliss and Sibley 1988, 14). Mickey Mouse, developed shortly after Disney's meeting with Mintz, brought worldwide acclaim and proved an immediate fillip after the Oswald episode. Yet, from this point forth, Disney's attitude towards the control and management of his Studio and its products changed irrevocably, resulting in the creation of a carefully regulated self-image.

Crucially, readings of this image have, in many ways, been guided by Disney itself. Volumes such as *The Illusion of Life: Disney Animation* (Thomas and Johnson, 1995), *Walt Disney: An American Original* (Thomas, 1994), *Work in Progress: Risking Failure, Surviving Success* (Eisner, 1999) and *Walt Disney's Nine Old Men and the Art of Animation* (Canemaker, 2001), released by Disney's Hyperion and Disney Editions publishing houses, valorize the efforts of the Studio's imagineers and management. The family-sanctioned biography *The Story of Walt Disney* (1956), by Diane Disney Miller (written in conjunction with Pete Martin), while originating from a non-Disney publisher, provides perhaps the earliest example of this trend.

Similarly, editions such as *The Art of The Lion King* (Finch, 1995a), *The Art of Hercules: The Chaos of Creation* (Rebello, 1997a), *The Art of the Hunchback of Notre Dame* (Rebello, 1997b), *The Art of Mulan* (Kurtti, 1998), *Treasure Planet: A Voyage of Discovery* (Kurtti, 2002) and *The Art of The Princess and the Frog* (Kurtti, 2009) extend this strategy in a film-specific manner. While these texts do provide a range of excellent concept, pre-production and production stage stills, because of their fan orientation they do not engage critically, for any length of time, with the material presented.

This strategy of control is also visible in the Studio's VHS, DVD and now Blu-ray release strategies. Unlike most mainstream Hollywood studios, Disney chooses to limit when specific titles re-enter circulation and for how long they will remain available. This strategy serves a dual purpose, both increasing the exclusivity – and prestige – of a title and also ensuring demand for the product when it is finally released (usually in the lead-up to a major holiday season). Additionally, Disney recently produced the DVD series *Walt Disney Treasures*, which, while offering an opportunity to view rare, early animations, also provides a way to recommodify titles that would otherwise lie dormant in the Studio's media archive. The presence of film historian Leonard Maltin, who introduces each of the *Walt Disney Treasures* editions, also serves to validate the series critically.

Lastly, access to Disney's comprehensive archive in Burbank, California, is severely restricted at present – a significant hurdle for any current Disney researcher. In recent years, only those working on sanctioned studies (such as Neal Gabler's *Walt Disney: The Triumph of the American Imagination* [2006]) have been granted entry. Certain documents, Michael Barrier writes, 'are not yet available to researchers who have the company's blessing. Roy Disney's papers, made available to Bob Thomas for his biography, remain closed to most writers, as do materials with continuing legal significance (in what are called the "main files")' (2008, xii). Furthermore, Barrier postulates, if such a thing 'as a "definitive" biography of Walt Disney is even possible, it will be decades before it can be written' (2008, xii).

In the absence of independent access, the regulated texts, *The Disney that Never Was: The Stories and Art of Five Decades of Unproduced Animation* (Solomon, 1995), *Before the Animation Begins: The Art and Lives of Disney Inspirational Sketch Artists* (Canemaker, 1996), *Paper Dreams: The Art And Artists Of Disney Storyboards* (Canemaker, 1999) and *Walt Disney Animation Studios, The Archive Series: Story* (Anonymous, 2008), provide the best glimpse into the Disney Archives. Whereas the Disney-sanctioned books, carefully calculated release strategy and archival DVD compendiums promote and protect a coherent concept of Disney animation, by contrast, independent scholarly research pertaining to Disney remains uneven.

Perhaps the most worrying consequence of this strategy of control and self-promotion is the Disney-centric appreciation of animation, and animation history, which has found purchase within popular culture. Online media, in many cases circumventing editorial processes and peer review, have multiplied assertions about Disney's perceived parentage of animation as an art form. Search engines, which feed off these statements, effectively reinforce this misconception; a Google search of the phrase 'father of animation', performed on 1 September 2010, returned 'Quotes from Walt Disney: The Father of Animation', as the most relevant result. Similarly, the Studio's contribution to the development of sound and colour technology, within the medium of animation, is often overestimated and misinterpreted. Janet Wasko writes: 'Only a few of Walt Disney's biographers attempt to establish any context for the company's achievements. Indeed, many profiles give him so much credit for animation innovations that one would think that animation originated with Walt Disney' (2001, 21).

By focusing primarily on the Studio's feature-length animation, namely the fifty, theatrically released, animated features identified on the 'History' page of the official *Walt Disney Animation Studios* website (see the Filmography subsection 'Disney's Animated Features' for a complete list of these 'prestige' releases), this book represents a critical intervention that seeks not only to interrogate the aforementioned misconceptions, but also to bring scholarly definition to those aspects of contemporary Disney (such as the Disney 'Renaissance' and the 'Neo-Disney' period) that remain relatively neglected. Furthermore, given the multifaceted nature of Disney, discussion will be necessarily multidisciplinary, combining economic, cultural, historical, textual and technological approaches.

This book, therefore, is divided into three parts: *Re-examining Disney*, *Early and Middle Disney Feature Animation* and *Contemporary Disney Feature Animation*. In the first part, Chapters 1 and 2 seek to provide the reader with a more nuanced understanding of Disney authorship and Disney's contribution to the development of animation technology and practice, with particular emphasis placed on sound, colouration and the multiplane camera. In *Early and Middle Disney Feature Animation*, the focus shifts to rethinking how Disney is perceived. It has been said that mass culture relies on replication, that 'content, ideological schema, the blurring of contradictions – these are repeated, but the superficial forms are varied' (Barthes 1975, 41). Disney's animated features, which are often taken as microcosmic reflections of this disposition, have come to be viewed homogeneously as a canonical body. Chapter 3, therefore, develops a critical alternative to the now overdetermined term 'Classic Disney', by introducing the concept of Disney-Formalism, which provides a new theoretical and historical framework with which to read Disney feature animation. Chapter 4 provides both a historical and textual analysis of the surrealist short *Destino* (2003) – a short which problematizes homogeneous readings of the Studio as a producer of purely conventional and conservative animation. Concluding the part, Chapter 5 examines the evolution that took place at the Studio during the 1970s and 1980s – a factor that is sometimes deemphasized in contemporary studies of Disney. In *Contemporary Disney Feature Animation*, the emphasis is placed on bringing definition to recent Disney. Chapter 6, therefore, provides an analysis of the Disney Renaissance, which, despite being an established concept (signifying a body of artistically revitalized films that spanned the years 1989 to 1999), does not yet occupy a prominent position in studies of Disney. Moving beyond this, Chapter 7 focuses on the artistic deviations that characterize the Studio's post-millennial productions; this Neo-Disney period, as it is termed, is perhaps the most marginalized of all the phases in Disney's evolution. Lastly, Chapter 8 discusses the Disney–Pixar relationship, considering to what extent the latter's films and personnel have helped shape the former's creative direction.

Part 1

Re-examining Disney

Chapter 1

Disney Authorship

Introduction

The Sorcerer's Apprentice is one of Disney's most iconic animated sequences. It tells the story of an impetuous apprentice – Mickey Mouse – who seeks to use his master's magic to make his domestic work easier. After seeing the sorcerer leave for bed, Mickey dons his master's hat, interpreting it as the source of his powers, and proceeds to bring a wooden broom to life. Having done so, Mickey then instructs the broom to fill the basement's basin with water from an outside fountain; witnessing the broom's mastery of this task allows Mickey to relax, which quickly sees him fall asleep. However, while he rests, the broom continues to fill the indoor basin until it begins to overflow. Panicking, Mickey tries, ineffectively, to stop the broom, eventually attacking it with an axe. Unfortunately, the broken splinters become new brooms that, in turn, form a water-carrying army which relentlessly fills the basement with water. As Mickey floats upon the Sorcerer's spell book, frantically searching for an incantation to stop the brooms, his predicament becomes increasingly perilous as a whirlpool begins to pull him beneath the surface. At this moment the Sorcerer appears at the basement entrance. Gesturing, he parts the water and descends. With the water receding, Mickey bashfully returns the magic hat to his master and continues with the housework by hand.

Most viewers would probably identify Mickey Mouse as the sole perpetrator of this chaos. Such a response, however, reveals the difficulty of studying authorship. Romantic notions of authorship, such as William Wordsworth's definition of poetic authorship as a 'spontaneous overflow of powerful feelings' (1984, 598) recollected in tranquillity, no longer offer a satisfactory account of the authorial process. Roland Barthes' essay, 'The Death of the Author', provides perhaps the most famous counterpoint, arguing that a 'text is a tissue of quotations drawn from the innumerable centres of culture' (1995, 128). Although Mickey may be the most visible authorial force in the aforementioned sequence, this belies the numerous converging factors that both support and are shaped by his vision – most notably the broom, the hat and the Sorcerer.

Disney's role in the 'authorship' of his animated features is no less complex. As Sean Griffin notes, 'Walt Disney so successfully performed authorship of his studio's output during his lifetime that many customers thought Walt drew all the cartoons himself' (2000, 141). Worryingly, this oversimplified appreciation of Disney authorship can still be seen today, perpetuated, as noted in the Introduction, through internet forum posts and similarly critically unregulated spaces. If we return once more to *The Sorcerer's Apprentice*, it is possible to view the short allegorically, representing specific tenets of Disney authorship: Mickey reflects Disney's desire to innovate, to find new ways of producing animation; the broom, a paragon of hard work, which, in its fractured state, becomes an efficient work force, symbolizes the hierarchical evolution that occurred at the Studio as Disney pursued an industrialized model of cartoon production; the hat, emblematic of the Sorcerer's magic, functions much in the same manner as Disney's name, serving to prime audience expectation; and lastly, the Sorcerer, a figure of power, mirrors Disney's omniscience during his Studio's 'Golden Age'. Given this complexity, it will be useful, in this opening chapter, to detail how 'Disney's' authorship evolved during his stewardship, and to explore the possibility that other figures within the Studio might hold competing claims to authorship of 'Disney's' animated features.

Authorial Evolution

Clearly, Disney constitutes a rather unconventional authorial figure. The collaborative nature of film, which in recent years has come to represent the biggest challenge to the auteur concept, is even more pronounced when discussing feature animation. In addition to the compartmentalized nature of animation production, in which hierarchically and topographically separate artists work towards a unifying goal, the Studio, by 1935, 'had more than 250 employees' (Barrier 2008, 110). However, this vision of Disney production, which problematizes a simple attribution of authorship, is reconciled by Disney himself: 'I think of myself as a little bee. I go from one area of the Studio to another, and gather pollen and sort of stimulate everybody . . . that's the job I do' (Schickel 1997, 33).

Central to this 'bee' analogy is Disney's disengagement from the actual physical act of animation, which had been a facet of Disney production since the late 1920s. Disney has himself remarked on this transition:

I started as an artist in 1919. And I actually did my first animated films in early 1920. And at that time I drew everything, painted every background and things. And I carried along as an animator and an artist until about the time of Mickey Mouse. Now when Mickey Mouse came along there was such a demand – he made quite a splash – it was necessary then for me to give up on the drawing in order to organise and run the organisation. (Wells 2002b, 78–9

This was how Disney functioned for the majority of his stewardship, operating as, to borrow Paul Wells's definition, an extra-textual auteur; while Disney did not draw the key frames and in-betweens, or even ink the image, he was the 'person who prompt[ed] and execut[ed] the core themes, techniques and expressive agendas of a film' (2002b, 79). The production of *Snow White and the Seven Dwarfs* (1937) provides a good example of this type of authorship in action.

Michael Barrier observes that although 'Disney had started the year planning to direct *Snow White* himself . . . he was by the fall of 1936 delegating to [David] Hand a supervisory role over the whole of *Snow White*' (1999, 212–13). Given that much was resting on *Snow White*'s ability to return a profit, the election of Hand to effectively direct the project was a calculated decision. Hand 'approached the director's job in the spirit of a business executive, farming out detail work . . . to subordinates and concentrating instead on broader issues, which at the Disney studio entailed primarily an intensive reading of Walt Disney himself' (Barrier 1999, 134). Barrier uses 'reading' as a way of alluding to Hand's need, and ability, to gauge how best to please Disney. However, Hand's proclivity towards a broader level of control over *Snow White*, and his reluctance to involve himself in the daily artisanal tasks of the project, resulted in certain aspects of the film becoming fragmented.

One such issue revolved around how the dwarfs were to be realized. While it had been common practice in the years leading up to *Snow White* for animators to be assigned a particular character to animate (for example Art Babbitt's animation of Goofy), this appropriation of resources was impractical given the scale of *Snow White* and the numerous overlapping characters. Hand once remarked, with reference to the dwarfs, 'There were so many of the damn little guys running around, and you couldn't always cut from one to the other . . . We had to cut to groups of three and four, so it became a terrific problem of staging' (Barrier 1999, 244). Early in 1936 Hand came up with an alternative to the one-animator-to-one-character model, breaking the animation down, more or less, by sequence. To combat the lack of continuity inherent in this procedure, Hand called for 'each dwarf [to have] obvious mannerisms, so that they would be recognisable even in the least accomplished animation' (Barrier 1999, 214). Babbitt, however, argued against such superficial mannerisms as a way to define character, calling for animators to adopt a Stanislavskian mindset: 'You have to go deeper . . . You have to go inside – how he [the character] feels' (Barrier 1999, 214). Ultimately, the solution to this conflict came via live action. By filming actors (and Studio staff) to form unique character 'maps' for each dwarf, when individual animators were called to animate a particular dwarf, they had a quick reference point, which could refresh the specific mechanics of that character.

While this situation was effectively resolved by a handful of the Studio's more senior personnel without Disney's direct intervention, this belies the authorial influence he did exert. This can be seen, first and foremost, in the fact that continuity of appearance *was* such an important issue. Disney's insistence on carefully planned scenarios and industrially executed animation constitute key predicates on which *Snow White* was made, and an absolute insistence on continuity is one of the most visible ways in which Disney's animation differs from earlier examples of 'straight ahead' animation (see Chapter 2). Secondly, and perhaps most significantly, the key animators' awareness of Disney's instance on believability would have guided them, as Babbitt remarked, to get 'inside' the dwarfs' minds. This insistence on 'verisimilitude in . . . characters, contexts and narratives' (Wells 1998, 23) during the production of *Snow White* effectively established the blueprint for what would become the Disney-Formalist style (see Chapter 3) – a style that dominated the Studio for several years.

Given that Disney's name now connotes and promotes much more than just squash-and-stretch animation, Wells has also argued that the 'Disney' name be redefined 'as a metonym for *an authorially complex, hierarchical industrial process, which organises and executes selective practices within the vocabularies of animated film*' (2002c, 140). This appropriation of 'Disney' is a particularly appealing one considering the persistence and mutability of Disney's authorship, beginning in the 1920s, running throughout the 'Golden Age', and continuing after his death in 1966. Furthermore, 'Disney' has become a signifier for a particular way of reading 'a film, or series of films, with coherence and consistency, over-riding all the creative diversity, production processes, socio-cultural influences and historical conditions et cetera which may challenge this perspective' (Wells 2002b, 76). In this sense, Disney serves as a trigger, priming the audience to expect a specific style of animation, be it produced during the 'Golden Age' or more recently, during the Studio's Renaissance period (see Chapter 6).

This interrogation of the complexities of Disney authorship, and the industrial processes that support it, provides a welcome alternative to Marc Eliot's troubling and controversial account of Disney authorship. At his most progressive, Eliot proposes a romanticized notion of Disney author-ship, positioning Disney at the centre of all filmic meaning – a version of authorship far removed from that of the cross-pollinating bee, whose main responsibility is to unite the creative individuals who are physically respon-sible for the finished animation. Taking *The Three Caballeros* (1944) as an example, Eliot sees the film's colourful aesthetic and amorous Donald Duck (Figure 1.1), as 'the most vivid representation yet of Disney's raging unconscious' (2003, 180). Most alarming, however, is how Eliot's account ignores the social context in which the film was produced – a factor which would have had a definite influence on the film's animators.

FIGURE 1.1   An amorous Donald Duck.

Ultimately, Eliot sees *The Three Caballeros* as a direct reflection of Disney's own personal feelings and mental state, pointing to how, during the production of *The Three Caballeros*, '[John Edgar] Hoover was feeding Walt a continuous stream of information regarding the possibility of his Spanish heritage' (2003, 180). Eliot argues that at the 'same time the *true* facts of his birth were being investigated, Disney "gave birth" to Donald Duck, in many ways Walt's "second-born" and Mickey Mouse's antithetical "sibling"' (2003, 180, emphasis added). Eliot even goes so far as to interpret the Mickey Mouse and Donald Duck characters in a psychoanalytical context:

> Clearly, Disney regarded Mickey and Donald as more than just animated characters. They were, in many ways, his most important progeny, over which he maintained absolute creative control in projecting his own, conflicted personality: Mickey as superego – humble, chaste, cerebral, asexual, always in control, universally adored; Donald as id – darker, volatile, emotional, sexual, always out of control, not quite as popular and angry because of it. (2003, 181–2)

Eliot concludes that Disney's decision to 'retire' Mickey Mouse for *The Three Caballeros* had less to do with market demand, and more to do with Disney's personal emotions: 'Mickey's absence may have signalled the breakdown of Walt's fragile emotional balance, projected in the emergence of an unleashed Donald, the sexually provocative, libidinous duck, who thumped with desire for all make and manner of *unattainable Spanish women*' (2003, 182).

By contrast, Esther Leslie comments, with reference to the production of *The Three Caballeros*: 'The loss of [stylistic] unity is symptomatic; that is to say, it is true to the epoch. The film reflects the deep bewilderment of the time, a time of war. Disney comes yet again to be a symptom of the crisis of culture, and the crisis of the social world, yet this time negatively, without hope. Disney is absorbent of the prevailing energies' (2004, 291). While the precise sociohistorical conditions highlighted by Leslie would undoubtedly have coloured the animator's artistic choices at this time, other, more pragmatic, influences would also have had an impact on the collaborative process required to produce such a film.

Given the obvious attraction, yet inaccuracy, of such accounts of Disney authorship, Wells's redefinition of Disney as metonym provides an essential, industry-centred paradigm through which to interpret Disney authorship. While Wells observes that Disney is 'an auteur by virtue of fundamentally denying inscription to anyone else, and creating an identity and a mode of representation which, despite cultural criticism, market variations, and changing social trends, transcends the vicissitudes of contemporary America' (2002b, 90), he does not seek to recover the authorial claims of those subsumed by the Disney name. Instead, his multi-purpose redefinition serves to 'prioritise an address of the aesthetic agendas of the Disney canon in preference to ideological debates' (Wells 2002b, 85).

However, Disney's investment in the authorial process changed throughout his life, ranging from his well-documented omnipotence during the Studio's 'Golden Age', to a more reticent involvement through the late 1950s and up until his death in 1966. His authorial commitment during the earlier period is particularly evident in a series of memos sent in June 1935. As Barrier notes, Disney sent these 'memoranda to thirteen of his animators, criticizing their work individually' (2008, 112). One animator, Bob Wickersham, received the following comments:

It has been observed that you lack an understanding of the proper portrayal of gags. The development of showmanship is a valuable thing and plays a great part in one's analytical ability. Your sense of timing is limited and needs to be developed. Likewise, your resourcefulness in handling a personality has need of improvement. . . . Don't lose sight of the fact that confusion at any point in a scene's progress, be it on your board or the assistant's or the inkers, makes for loss of time and an increase in animation cost. (Barrier 2008, 113)

Such micromanagement, representative of Disney's own bee analogy, contrasts starkly with his involvement in the Studio's animation from the mid-1950s onwards. In the years following World War II, 'Disney's interest in animation waned as he increasingly turned his attention to live-action movies, nature documentaries, television, and the planning of his innovative amusement park' (Watts 1995, 95). Moreover, Barrier observes:

Consumed by his roles as proprietor of an amusement park and overseer of a studio churning out mediocre live-action movies, Walt Disney had surrendered his role as artist. There is sometimes the sense, in the recollections of people who worked with him on his best films and were still on his staff in the 1950s, that their presence could be an annoying reminder of what he had left behind. (2008, 269)

This disengagement had a profound effect on Disney's attitude towards his Studio's short animation. No longer was he concerned, above all else, with the quality of his art; now his priority was quantity. Confronted with the realities of television scheduling, Disney drew a startling analogy: 'Once you are in television, it's like operating a slaughter house. Nothing must go to waste. You have to figure ways to make glue out of the hoofs' (Schumach 1961).

Reitherman's Eight Old Men

The influence of Disney's 'Nine Old Men', a group of senior animators (Les Clark, Marc Davis, Ollie Johnston, Milt Kahl, Ward Kimball, Eric Larson, John Lounsbery, Wolfgang Reitherman and Frank Thomas) who had been at Disney since the 1930s, provides perhaps the clearest example of an authorial other within the Studio's animated canon. While not the originators of the Studio's principles and techniques of character animation, these Nine Old Men 'developed and refined those methods to a high degree of expressiveness and subtlety over a forty-year period' (Canemaker 2001, vii). Steven Watts offers the following summary of the individual strengths of this group:

> Clark, the senior member of the group, was a quiet and skilled draftsman . . . Reitherman, a man of enormous energy and determination, threw himself into every line he drew and revised his work endlessly. Larson displayed great flexibility and sympathy as an artist . . . Kahl was an intense, blunt man whose brilliant clarity of drawing matched his irascible personality. Thomas, an exacting animator given to research and careful thinking about his craft, brought an attention to detail and a concern with motivation that added complexity to his characters. Johnson's drawings possessed a natural appeal, focusing on acting, and he had a feel for emotion that practically defined personality animation. Lounsbery, an introverted craftsman, developed a loose, energetic, and bold style . . . Davis, the renaissance man of the group, had a flair for the dramatic and animated characters, designed scenes, and worked in story development for many Disney movies over the years. Finally, Kimball was a flamboyant and colourful artist whose tastes ran to unexpected and satirical humour, sharp mimicry, and surrealism. (1997, 267)

The authorial claims of this group were given credibility in 1972 when the Studio's 'publicity department perpetuated and built the legend of the Nine Old Men with a . . . group photograph' (Canemaker 2001, vii). This posed picture, which depicts the men very much as a team, with a seated row of four backed by a standing row of five, 'was an attempt to personalize the continuation of the art form that Walt developed by shining a spotlight on his closest, most loyal, and gifted collaborators' (Canemaker 2001, vii). However, as John Canemaker notes in his study, *Walt Disney's Nine Old Men and the Art of Animation*, 'the term obscured the individual achievements of nine unique talents and temperaments, even as it purportedly illuminated them' (2001, vii). Of this group it was Reitherman who arguably held the greatest authorial claim over the Studio's animation during Disney's period of distraction.

With films such as *The Sword in the Stone* (1963), *The Jungle Book* (1967), *The Aristocats* (1970) and *Robin Hood* (1973), Reitherman, in his directorial capacity, worked to reconcile the stylistic needs of the Xerox process (see Chapter 5) with the traditions of Disney-Formalist animation. This period, lasting roughly twelve years, provides one of the strongest claims for an identifiable authorial presence, other than Disney, within the Studio's feature animation. In fact, Reitherman's contribution during this time *has* prompted animation enthusiasts to discuss Reitherman's stylistic influence on these films, particularly *Robin Hood*, rather than as seeing them solely as 'Disney' works.

Mark Mayerson's internet blog, *Mayerson on Animation: Reflections on the Art and Business of Animation*, is one such site of critical confluence, featuring comment from animation enthusiasts and aficionados, and industry practitioners past and present. The article 'Reitherman Reruns' proves most relevant, as it both prompts and features arguments for an identifiable, Reitherman-specific disposition within Disney feature animation during his directorial tenure: animation reuse. This technique sees images, animation cycles, and movement timings, among other things, adapted from an earlier production for use in a new one. It is a common practice for economically challenged studios, whose main priority is the timely delivery of an animated television serial, to keep libraries of their most common character and background animations to enhance productivity. While this tactic is not often associated with Disney animation, the films directed by Reitherman reveal a clear inclination towards it.

Rather than being merely a reflection of the budget restrictions of that period, Floyd Norman – an animator on several of Reitherman's productions, Disney Legend inductee and current e-journalist – claims that 'Reuse was just Woolie's thing' (2009). Norman's view is consolidated by the fact that animation reuse can be seen in Reitherman's directorial work as early as 1957 (Lionel 2009), such as in the animated short *The*

Truth About Mother Goose. After the short's initial storybook opening, Jack Horner is shown delivering a pie. When compared side-by-side with the first appearance of J. Worthington Foulfellow in *Pinocchio* (1940), Horner's swaying walk cycle replicates that of Foulfellow. *The Truth About Mother Goose* was made shortly after *Lady and the Tramp* (1955). Considering that *Lady and the Tramp*, having been produced for approximately $4 million, grossed $8.3 million, it is probable that *The Truth About Mother Goose* would have had adequate financial support during production. This earlier example of reuse complicates the view that Reitherman's features of the 1960s and 1970s reused animation for purely budgetary reasons, and it supports the view that, in fact, it reflects a recurrent artistic tendency.

Mayerson's article features a short video compilation that cuts between examples of original animation and Reitherman's reuse of it. Consequently, many of the responses either focus on Reitherman's motivations for, or the implications of, reusing earlier animation. For the most part, these responses can be divided into three categories: those that dislike this practice ('No matter what the circumstance . . . it's pretty damn lazy' [Semaj 2009]), those that see it as a necessary cost-cutting measure ('the reason *Reitherman* recycled the old animation was time and budget' [Pat 2009, emphasis added]), and those, like Norman, who see it more as a product of artistic choice. Ultimately, these disparate opinions all share in an impassioned discussion of one specific aspect of Reitherman's authorial style – *his* reuse of animation. In fact, during the course of the debate, the proper nouns 'Woolie' and Reitherman (and their possessive alternatives) feature a total of forty times. In comparison, the proper nouns Disney (referring to Walt Disney the man) and Walt (and their possessive alternatives) feature only twelve times. References to Reitherman's authorship, in what is ostensibly a debate about *Disney* animation, outnumber references to Disney by almost four to one, highlighting that it is possible for a figure other than Disney to provoke sustained and serious debate concerning authorship within the Studio's animated canon.

Reitherman's greatest authorial claim lies in his stewardship of the Studio's feature animation following the death of Disney. Determined, respected by his peers and an esteemed figure of authority to the younger animators, Reitherman fulfilled many of the roles vacated by Disney – albeit with little public recognition. Although featuring prominently in the 'Nine Old Men' photograph of 1972, he remains part of the collective. However, while only the formal group photograph was intended for public release, another is chosen by Canemaker as a frontispiece for his study of the 'Nine Old Men'. Semantically, this other photograph presents an interesting scene: Disney's 'Nine' have now become Reitherman's 'Eight'. Flanked by the other eight 'Old Men', Reitherman, now standing alone at the front of the group, occupies the most important position within Disney feature animation production: that which was vacated by Disney himself – heading the group of animators, leading them forward; visibly engaging with the storyboard, directing them towards a cohesive vision; operating as a conduit of control between creativity and creation.

Conclusion

Although more nuanced readings of Disney authorship have been made possible since Disney's death, through such means as director's commentaries and internet fan sites, authorial figures, such as Reitherman, did exist during Disney's stewardship and thus deserve recognition. As later chapters will illustrate, individuals such as Michael Eisner and John Lasseter have also commanded significant control over the creative direction of Disney feature animation, but with differing outcomes. While this opening chapter has focused on Disney's centrality, as an individual, to the authorship process within his Studio, a similarly revisionist approach is required when considering how Disney the studio, as industrial participant, dominates the narrative of early American animation.

Chapter 2

A History of Innovation?

Introduction

If you were to ask 'the man on the street' who the father of animation was, 'you are likely to hear the name Walt Disney' (Beck 2004, 12). Although this view has never been formally endorsed by the Disney Studio, it is easy to see how such a misconception might arise. Dominic Rushe, for example, writing in *The Sunday Times*, once asserted that 'Walt Disney was the founding father of animation', and that, with films such as '*Bambi* [1941], *Cinderella* [1950] and *Snow White and the Seven Dwarfs* [1937], Disney created a whole new genre of movies' (2003). This statement is troubling for two reasons. First, Disney, with the films identified by Rushe, did not create a new genre of movie as such; rather, the Studio helped to establish and popularize a new mode of animation (see Chapter 3). Secondly, between the releases of *Snow White* and *Bambi*, the Fleischer Studios released two animated features, *Gulliver's Travels* (1939) and *Mr. Bug Goes to Town* (1941), which, without the help of Disney, helped to consolidate the concept of feature-length animation – the new genre to which Rushe may be alluding. Ultimately, it is the unqualified identification of Disney as *the* 'founding father' of animation that is most disconcerting.

Clearly, Disney is not *the* founding father of animation; in fact, there are other, well-established candidates with more tangible claims to that title. J. Stuart Blackton, with *Humorous Phases of Funny Faces* (1906), refined the area of profilmic spectacle, matching the edges of the lightning sketcher's canvas (a blackboard) to the limit of the camera's aperture, and effectively gave birth to the animated world. Émile Cohl created the first metamorphic, yet identifiable, animated protagonist in *Fantasmagorie* (1908). Winsor McCay, with *Gertie the Dinosaur* (1914), took character animation further still, endowing his prehistoric star with a recognizable personality. McCay also achieved an early high point in individual artistic expression with *The Sinking of the Lusitania* (1918), which required himself and his assistant John Fitzsimmons to make 'twenty-five thousand drawings' (Sito 2006, 9) over a twenty-two month period. Finally, John Randolph Bray, a passionate industrialist of animation practices, developed *Colonel Heeza Liar in Africa* (1913), which is considered by many to be 'the first commercial-cartoon release' (Maltin 1987, 7), and which prompted the first cartoon serialization. In this respect, not only did Bray's *Colonel Heeza Liar* series establish a paradigm that *Felix the Cat* (1919–30) would later build upon, but the notion of a cartoon series itself was something that Disney benefitted from with the likes of *Oswald the Lucky Rabbit* (1927–43), *Mickey Mouse* (1928–99) and the *Silly Symphonies* (1929–39).

While the contributions made by such pioneers predate Disney's work within American animation, during the first half of the twentieth century Disney and his Studio did play an important part in developing many of the features and principles of mainstream animation. Although a teleological argument could be constructed to account for this, one that draws on Disney's evolution from amateur lightning sketch artist to industrializing figurehead, it is important to acknowledge Disney's fortune of being 'the right person at the right time'. Ironically, it is perhaps because of Disney's late entrance to the animation industry that his name is so strongly identified with the form, given that many of animation's pioneers had a tendency to self-destruct. As Alan Bryman observes, Bray 'relied too much on patent protection for his studio's success; [Raoul] Barré fell out with his partner . . . and [Pat] Sullivan suffered from the most common malaise among successful pioneers, complacency' (1997, 434). In contrast to this, Disney, as a late entrant, was able 'to capitalise on the achievements of Bray and the early entrants' (Bryman 1997, 433). In addition to embracing Taylorist methods of management and borrowing technologically from the pioneers, Disney coupled a perpetual desire to innovate (leading to differentiation through sound and colour technologies) with 'an obsessive attention to detail' (Bryman 1997, 428). Therefore, by the time Disney released *Steamboat Willie* (1928), he had effectively surpassed pioneers such as Bray, inheriting an audience familiar with – and hungry for – short animation, yet unprepared for the technological developments he had recently harnessed.

In addition to being central to the Studio's early success, the Mickey Mouse creation myth captures in microcosm the popular tendency to misread certain aspects of the Studio's early evolution. After losing control of *Oswald the Lucky Rabbit* (1927–28), Mickey Mouse represented the ideal response, being the perfect character to compete with the likes of Oswald and *Felix the Cat* (The Pat Sullivan Studio, c.1919–30). Accounts of Mickey's exact origin, however, are less well-defined. Disney claims that while returning to the West Coast from New York (after meeting with Charles Mintz of Winkler Productions), he had, in his mind, 'dressed [his] dream mouse in a pair of red velvet pants with two huge pearl buttons, had composed the first scenario and was all set' to begin animating (Schickel 1997, 116). Other accounts suggest that it was Iwerks who, upon hearing that *Oswald the Lucky Rabbit* had been lost, resourcefully found a way to counter Mintz's strategy. Dave Iwerks, son of Ub Iwerks, argues that 'Mickey was Ub's character' (Eliot 2003, 36). He does concede that Disney did showcase a mouse character to his father; however, this mouse was called Mortimer and overtly resembled Disney – Mickey only shared Disney's voice. Although Iwerks *can* be credited with the visual creation of Mickey, the 'many mice that had appeared in earlier silent cartoons and the . . . popular *Felix the Cat*' had an obvious influence on Mickey's visual construction (Solomon 1995, 6). Essentially, 'ear shapes distinguished one round character from another; remove pointed ears and add two long oblong ones and Felix became a Rabbit named Oswald; substitute two round circles, and Oswald begat a mouse named Mickey' (Canemaker 1996, 4).

This competition between a history promoted and prized by the Studio and one supported by external accounts – microcosmically reflected in the story of Mickey Mouse's conception – underpins much of the early Disney mythos. This chapter, therefore, seeks to examine this historical double helix, concentrating on Disney's depiction as an industrializing figure; the Studio's contribution to the development of sound cartoons, the film soundtrack and stereo sound; the Studio's role in the advancement of colour animation; and the origins of Disney's multiplane camera.

Straight Ahead versus Pose to Pose

During animation's 'Golden Age' the Studio was instrumental in formalizing a number of principles. These principles covered a range of topics relating to the act of animation itself and reflect, through their formalized existence, Disney's perpetual desire to industrialize. As Sergei Eisenstein's theories have led the Russian theorist and filmmaker to become synonymous with Soviet montage, often to the occlusion of his compatriot filmmakers, Disney's synonymy with particular animation mechanics – outlined in Frank Thomas and Ollie Johnson's 1981, Hyperion-published, *Disney Animation: The Illusion of Life* (revised and reprinted in 1995 as *The Illusion of Life: Disney Animation*) – has led to a similar obfuscation of animation prior to, and contemporaneous with, Disney's 'Golden Age' output. The publication of these principles by Thomas and Johnson has served to centralize Disney's perceived contribution to the evolution of animation style and industrial practice. Marc Davis, commenting on this period, adds further weight to this view, stating: 'What we [Disney's animators] were in on, really, was the invention of animation' (Eisen 1975, 41). Such has been the impact of Thomas and Johnson's text that even handbooks for computer animation refer to it as the 'main source for the principles of animation' (Adams, Miller and Sims 2004, 508). Only recently have significant, critically minded studies (*Understanding Animation* [Wells 1998], *The Animator's Survival Kit: A Manual of Methods, Principles and Formulas for Classical, Computer, Games, Stop Motion and Internet Animators* [Williams 2001] and *The Fundamentals of Animation* [Wells 2006]) on the mechanics of traditional animation emerged to offer an alternative to Thomas and Johnson's study.

Thomas and Johnson outline twelve basic mechanical principles of animation: squash and stretch, anticipation, staging, straight ahead action and pose to pose, follow through and overlapping action, slow in and slow out, arcs, secondary action, timing, exaggeration, solid drawing, and appeal (1995, 47). Primarily, these practices were encouraged because they added a sense of 'realism' to Disney's animation. On the development of these principles, Thomas and Johnson state: 'As each of these processes *acquired* a name, it was analyzed and *perfected* and talked about, and when *new* artists joined the staff they were taught these practices as if they were the rules of the trade. To everyone's surprise, they became the fundamental principles of animation' (1995, 47, emphasis added). This assertion is particularly revealing in that it shows how, in the Studio's opinion, the Disney doctrine came to dominate animation. Although oblique reference is made to the pre-existence of the listed processes, it was at Disney, according to Thomas and Johnson, where they *acquired* names and were *perfected*. Additionally, artists flocked to the Studio during the 'Golden Age', and that these new animators were taught the practices – 'as if they were the rules of the trade' (Thomas and Johnson 1995, 47) – would only have further served to disseminate Disney's animation doctrine.

When Thomas and Johnson discuss straight ahead and pose to pose animation, they are essentially making a claim for Disney's industrial innovation. In straight ahead animation 'the animator literally works straight ahead from his first drawing in the scene . . . getting new ideas as he goes along, until he reaches the end of the scene' (Thomas and Johnson 1995, 56). Contrastingly, with pose to pose animation, the animator plots the action, decides what drawings will be needed, creates the drawings, relating them to each other in dimension and action, and then gives the scene to his assistant to produce the in-betweens. In this model of animation, the main poses are established by a key animator, while 'other animators "in-betweened" the movement between them' (Wells 2002b, 25–6) – hence the term in-betweener. Clearly, pose to pose animation is the style most emblematic of Disney, symbolizing a measured, industrialized approach to animation that is in direct opposition, both practically and ideologically, to the spontaneous straight ahead style (a style which shares notable similarities with surrealism's automatism). Moreover, Thomas and Johnson claim that most 'of the animators who came from the East knew only Straight Ahead animation' (1995, 538). When coupled with Les Clark's assertion that 'Pose to Pose, as we knew it, was developed at . . . Disney' (Thomas and Johnson 1995, 538), these claims serve to consolidate the idea that the Studio was *the* major source of industrial innovation during the 'Golden Age'.

However, the animation team headed by Otto Messmer at The Pat Sullivan Studio may have utilized a form of pose to pose animation at a much earlier date. Although no explicit reference is made to the exact animation process employed by the studio, Leonard Maltin's observation that, by 1923, Sullivan had 'upped his output from twelve to twenty-six cartoons a year' (1987, 24), coupled with the studio's prototypical compartmentalization – visible in images of the studio's physical arrangement – suggests a predisposition towards organized production. Moreover, Messmer's multiple responsibilities, '*writing*, directing, and *partially* animating every film' (Maltin 1987, 24, emphasis added), further highlights the carefully prepared and executed nature of the studio's animation.

One of the greatest appeals of Sullivan's series was the Felix *character*. When creating *Felix the Cat*, Messmer, in his own words, placed a never-before-seen 'emphasis on personality' (Maltin 1987, 24). By developing personality in this way, and by actively promoting the character of Felix, the series grew in popularity, which in turn resulted in 'successful lines of merchandise and a newspaper cartoon strip' (Bryman 1997, 421). It is unlikely that such a consistent, focused and successful creation of personality could have relied solely on straight ahead principles of animation.

The indoctrinization of the twelve principles of animation, rather than consolidating a view of the Studio as an industrial innovator, instead indicates the Studio's awareness of the need to compete with the likes of Pat Sullivan's *Felix the Cat* and the Fleischer Studios's *Talkartoons* (1929–32). Disney's primary contribution at this time can be reduced to an identification of a demand for animation that developed personality and style together, and the practices formalized to meet this need.

Disney and the Coming of Sound Cartoons

Studies of the Studio often overlook how small it actually was at the beginning of the sound era, particularly in 'comparison with the corporate giants that controlled the film industry' (Wasko 2001, 12). Charles Solomon's account of Disney's role in the development of animation between 1928 and 1941, a period he labels 'The Disney Era', is indicative of this, stating that the industry's development from the silent era 'was largely achieved through the dedication, talent and vision of Walt Disney and the artists he employed. Virtually every tool and technique in the animator's repertoire was discovered, invented or perfected at the Disney studio during this era' (1994, 43). However, Disney needed emergent technologies, such as sound and colour, because his wish was not only to 'make films, but to make commercially viable films in a technologically advanced, modern industrial context, which could challenge the output of the established studios' (Wells 2002b, 80). In the face of financial hardship in 1928, Disney 'needed a novelty, and that novelty was sound. Sound had reached motion picture screens . . . with the release of *The Jazz Singer* [1927] . . . and Walt *decided* that sound would be a great *addition* to animated cartoons' (Smith and Clark 2002, 24, emphasis added).

The claim that it was Disney who first sought to *add* sound to animation – actively perpetuated by the Studio through Dave Smith and Steven Clark's *Disney: The First 100 Years* – is misleading. Moreover, the claim that Disney 'decided' to embrace sound pragmatically recasts the Studio's dependence on emergent technology. Similarly, Christopher Finch's coffee table study, *The Art of Walt Disney: from Mickey Mouse to the Magic Kingdoms* (1995b), contains only one dismissive reference to an earlier exponent of the sound cartoon: 'Max and Dave Fleischer had already produced a cartoon which used a . . . sound track, but . . . the experiment had had little impact on the industry' (Finch 1995b, 38). J. P. Telotte, in

The Mouse Machine: Disney and Technology (2008), understandably chooses to focus on the Studio's development of sound animation; however, while his coverage of Disney is comprehensive, he only briefly engages with earlier and competing advances in sound animation. Several pages into his chapter on Disney's development of sound, Telotte writes: 'While *Steamboat Willie* was not . . . the first Mickey Mouse cartoon – or even the first cartoon to employ sound – it is clearly the initial effort at designing a Mickey narrative with a consciousness of the various possibilities sound afforded' (Telotte 2008, 27). Unlike Finch, Telotte does not identify the Fleischer Studios as this earlier exponent of sound animation.

Richard Fleischer, son of Max Fleischer, points to *My Old Kentucky Home* (1924) – the first of the sound-tracked *Song Car-Tunes* – as the first true synchronized-sound short animation (2005, 43). However, a lack of public interest, and the fact that 'theatre owners thought it a basically impractical idea since special equipment was required to show the films' (Fleischer 2005, 43), brought the sound series to a premature end. Fleischer, although disappointed, still released the series as conventional silent shorts, having the satisfaction of knowing that he had produced the first sound cartoon (Fleischer 2005, 43–4).

Coming three years after the Fleischer Studios's first attempts at producing sound cartoons, *The Jazz Singer* 'thrilled audiences bored with the conventions of silent cinema and increasingly indifferent to the canned performances of the Vitaphone shorts' (Cook 2004, 210–11). However, from an artistic perspective, many of the directors and actors prominent during the silent era voiced antipathy towards the technological revolution. Not only did the introduction of sound remove the filmmaker from the poetic world of silent images, but, for a brief time, it also severely restricted potential camera movement. This was due to the fact that cameras designed for silent productions were still being used, and because of their operating noise, 'the camera and the cameramen were put in . . . soundproofed cubicles, weighing several tons, which were mounted on wheels and laboriously moved about the studio by hand' (Prendergast 1991, 20). Furthermore, even the hierarchy of filmmaking was momentarily reset during the early days of sound production. The director, who had previously commanded ultimate control over 'all aesthetic matters' during the silent era became subservient to the sound engineer, who, 'in the early days of sound . . . ruled supreme on set. No scene was shot without first consulting with him' (Prendergast 1991, 20). In contrast to this, facilitated by the rapid development of sound technology and unhindered by the limitations of early sound filming, Disney combined 'sound and image in an expressive manner impossible for his peers in live-action narrative cinema and . . . achieve[d] perfect frame-by-frame synchronization (today, the precise coordination of sound and image is still called "Mickey Mousing")' (Cook 2004, 233).

Steamboat Willie proved most ground-breaking in the way it precisely synchronized visual and acoustic stimuli, to the degree that one would become inseparable from the other. The combination of animation with music, both following a common rhythm, saw the Disney animators establish a new aesthetic: 'Instead of being a series of random effects, the cartoon achieved through music more solid structure than it had been possible to acquire from an unadorned story line' (Schickel 1997, 131). While *Steamboat Willie* provided a platform for this spectatorial pleasure to surface, *The Skeleton Dance* (1929) evolved this into something more. Through its narratological simplicity, aesthetic divergence and most importantly through its appropriation of classical music prêt-a-porter, *The Skeleton Dance* afforded Disney unanimous critical acceptance. Eisenstein observes:

> We are surprised by the harmony of the collective. By the harmony of technique . . . Disney's plastic visions, echoing the sounds, are captured *a priori*. Placed in a vise of the strictest plastic and temporal calculation. Made real. Coordinated by the dozens of hands of his collective. Shot on irreproachable rolls carrying charm, laughter and amazement at his virtuosity around the entire world. (1986, 2)

Although Eisenstein is effusive in praising Disney, it is appropriate that his commendation centres on the industrial aspects of Disney's sound productions, for ultimately this is where Disney's contribution to the development of sound rests – not as innovator, but as a producer whose works announced a newfound cohesion between animation and sound.

The Soundtrack

Although often overlooked, the construction and dissemination of the contemporary film soundtrack owes a lot to the opportunism of Disney at the time of *Snow White*'s exhibition. Before Victor Records released 'Songs From Walt Disney's *Snow White and the Seven Dwarfs*' (1938), the concept of a film soundtrack, comprised of original recordings from the film in question, was greeted with disdain.

As noted above, *The Jazz Singer* paved the way for sound film; however, film had been accompanied by sound since it was first projected, when 'the piano was used as much to cover up projector noise as to add any dramatic or aesthetic value to the moment' (Burlingame 2000, 1). While it took over a decade for full musical accompaniment to become commonplace, 'the audience of a silent film would very possibly hear a different accompaniment to the same film in a different cinema, or even from one screening to the next' (Davison 2004, 19). Despite this variation in content, in each performance the audience 'would hear a continuous musical accompaniment which bore a loose relationship to the narrative action' (Davison 2004, 19).

While the soundtrack, as it exists today, remained an alien concept to film producers during the silent era, by the mid-1920s they had started to appreciate the commercial value of film songs. Jon Burlingame writes:

> The vast majority of films continued to be silent, although exhibitors were by now accustomed to receiving full musical scores (played by pianists in the smaller houses, sometimes full orchestras in the big-city movie palaces) that occasionally incorporated popular songs. When savvy producers discovered that sheet music was a nifty marketing tool for their pictures – and sometimes produced a hit – they urged composers to incorporate tunes specifically written either for the score or as pure promotion for the picture. (2000, 1)

This resulted in a wave of film songs breaking into the popular music charts; among these were the songs 'Charmaine', from *What Price Glory* (1926), '(I'm in Heaven When I See You Smile) Diane', from *Seventh Heaven* (1927), and the hugely successful 'Ramona', from *Ramona* (1928).

As Burlingame notes, although *The Jazz Singer* redefined the concept of sound cinema, leading to the popularization of the 'all talking, all singing, all dancing' (2000, 1–2) film musical, nobody thought to recommodify the songs, as performed in the film, in the form of a phonographic record. This was largely because the profilmic song-and-dance performances, having been recorded live surrounded by attendant stage noise, were considered unsuitable for release as phonographic recordings. Furthermore, new '(and often shorter) versions were arranged and performed by bands and vocalists that the public knew and liked' (Burlingame 2000, 2).

Snow White broke with this model, becoming the first film to have an accompanying album produced 'utilizing the actual soundtracks recorded for the movie' (Smith and Clark 2002, 44). Much to Disney's delight, the songs 'I'm Wishing', 'Whistle While You Work', 'Heigh-Ho' and 'Some Day My Prince Will Come', showcased in the film, 'became not only hits, but standards' (Maltin 1987, 57). Adriana Caselotti, the voice artist for Snow White, also benefited from this change in sound-track policy, 'reaching *Billboard's* top 10 with "Some Day My Prince Will Come"' (Burlingame 2000, 2).

While the Studio did break the mould when they released the origi-nal soundtrack for *Snow White*, this did not immediately pave the way for other producers to follow suit. The iconic soundtracks of *The Adven-tures of Robin Hood* (1938), which won an Academy Award, and *Gone With the Wind* (1939), which received a nomination, both failed to make it into distribution because film music was still 'deemed neither classi-cal nor popular' (Burlingame 2000, 3). The main reason that Disney had the confidence to release the *Snow White* original soundtrack was because it was from a family film, and children's fare was considered marketable. The release of original soundtracks for both *Gulliver's Travels* (1939) and *Pinocchio* (1940) provides further evidence of this market force.

Although the original soundtrack had a faltering start, existing largely as a child-orientated product for several years, Disney played a key role in establishing it as it exists today. Furthermore, the soundtrack quickly became an important element of Disney's animated features, providing the perfect medium to extend the life of the Studio's most popular songs.

Stereo Sound: Fantasound

Within (live-action) film studies, it is widely considered that stereo sound was first popularized in the early 1950s to combat declining box-office receipts in the face of competition from television. Additionally, much of Orson Welles's early work is regarded by film scholars as representing the cinema's fledgling attempts at stereo sound, a view echoed by David Cook: 'In *Citizen Kane* [1941] he gave us the first modern sound film and effectively pioneered . . . stereophonic sound' (2004, 352). However, in 1940, Fantasound heralded a far greater departure from the existing methods of audio reproduction.

Disney, desperate to recreate the ambience of an orchestral perform-ance with his 'Concert Feature' (*Fantasia* [1940]), turned to William E. Garity and Leopold Stokowski to help accomplish this. Stokowski, reflecting on the development of Fantasound, remarks:

> Recording for motion pictures . . . cannot possibly sound exactly like the original because the original sounds from the orchestra came from a hundred different instruments and directions, whereas the reproduced music in the motion picture house comes from a relatively small number of sound diffusers or loudspeakers. In the original version of Fantasia we diffused the sound in two ways – one was from the back of the screen from three separate groups of loudspeakers – left, centre, right – the other was from loudspeakers all round the theatre . . . In Fantasia we had three separate sound channels, which put at our disposal several new possibilities. (Culhane 1983, 19)

While multiple musical sources had been recorded previously, the technology available restricted the playback potential. In his patent application for the Fantasound set-up, Garity makes the following observation concerning cinema acoustics: 'loud speaking means located behind the projection screen and the output level of each speaking means (if more than one is employed) is substantially uniform' (Garity and Hawkins 1940, 1). Fantasound, however, because of its multichannel, multispeaker capabilities, reproduced acoustics with a far greater precision than possible with the existing installations:

> When the sound waves of all . . . instruments are combined in a single channel, they often interfere with each other and cause cross-modulation, which makes the music sound distorted. With three separate channels, it is possible to send out the music on each channel from relatively few instruments. This reduces cross-modulation and gives greater purity to the sound of the instruments. Another great advantage of three sound channels is that the tone of various instruments can be blended in the air after the sound has left the speakers. (Culhane 1983, 19)

This aural cross-pollination was further enhanced by Fantasia's nine separate sound tracks and by the epic scale of the Fantasound installations, which featured an astounding '96 small speakers to pick up sound from one or more of the main [audio] channels' (Handzo 1985, 419). As Telotte summarizes, 'Fantasound was able to produce both a more naturalistic sound experience than in other sound films and fantastic aural effects through its capacity for isolating and manipulating individual sounds' (2008, 39).

Due to economic pressures, Disney's dream of Fantasound as *Fantasia's* standard acoustic installation was left unrealized, although where installations were sanctioned, his persistence with such an avant-garde method of music reproduction provided stereo dynamism for the then primitive sound cinema. This contribution was recognized in 1940 when an honorary Academy Award specifically championed his 'outstanding contribution to the advancement of the use of sound in motion pictures' ('Awards for Fantasia,' *The Internet Movie Database*). In this respect, Disney did truly break new ground technologically, anticipating both the work of Welles and the stereo cinema installations that occurred several decades later.

Colour

The Studio's contribution to the development of colour is another common area of misunderstanding. Despite the Studio's sophistication, efficiency and popular appeal, debt was still a major issue; even Disney's newfound marketability, visible in the mass-produced Mickey Mouse dolls, did little to keep the Studio in the black during a time of desperate economic depression. Disney knew that, both industrially and artistically, his studio was no longer alone at the top of the animation tree. In addition to Iwerks, who had left Disney in frustration over the fact that he was not getting the artistic credit he felt he deserved and was now heading the Pat Powers's financed Iwerks Studios, the Fleischer Studios also represented a serious challenge to Disney's long-term solvency. In 1932, prompted by the pressures of competition, Disney ventured to produce a colour *Silly Symphony*, utilizing a new colouration method developed by Technicolor.

Other colour technologies had existed prior to Technicolor's 1932 breakthrough three-colour process, for example, two-colour Kinemacolor, Kodachrome and Prizmacolor, and also a few three-colour processes, such as Chronochrome, Cinechrome and Zoechrome. Mechanically, the early two-colour methods relied on either an additive colouration or subtractive colouration process. In simple terms, the additive method saw green and red light recorded separately during the profilmic event, after which they were combined, in various measures, to produce the required colour. Contrastingly, the subtractive method achieved the required colour by 'extracting from white light all the unwanted wavelengths leaving only the colour required' (Happé 1971, 72).

However, these early two-colour processes reproduced only a fraction of the full colour spectrum, resulting in films that appeared excessively green or red. Furthermore, these processes also failed because they required 'substantial technological investment . . . generally increasing print costs far more than rentals could be expected to recoup' (Telotte 2008, 43).

Despite all the technological and financial obstacles, Disney's predecessors and competitors did endeavour to make use of the earlier processes. Powers, for example, 'who had . . . a bootleg sound process in the competitive days of early talkies . . . [arranged] to use the Cinecolor process' (Maltin 1987, 194). This agreement enabled Iwerks to make colour cartoons using a two-colour process. Cinecolor's two-colour process differed from that of the early two-colour Technicolor by using red and blue; this movement away from the red and green of two-colour Technicolor afforded 'greater possibilities, particularly for animated film' (Maltin 1987, 194). Leon Schlesinger Productions (formally Harman–Ising Productions [1930–33], which would latterly become Warner Bros. [1944–to date]), was another studio that embraced Cinecolor, buying into the technology as a way of moving into colour production, and seeing it as a means of gaining an advantage when 'promoting their films to theatre owners' (Maltin 1987, 229).

Bray Productions released a colour cartoon in 1920, entitled *The Debut of Thomas Cat*, which is widely held as the first American colour cartoon. Bray used an early two-colour process developed by Percy D. Brewster, named Brewster Color. The scope of Brewster's process was fairly advanced, and his patent application of 1917 refers to the use of two film strips coated in light sensitive emulsion, which 'may both be panchromatic' (Brewster 1917, 2). However, Brewster suggests having 'one sensitized chiefly for light of one or more colours above, say yellow-green of the spectrum, and the other for colours below yellow-green' (1917, 2). Despite the ambition of Brewster's colour process, Bray only used it once because 'the double-emulsion film was . . . susceptible to scratches' (Maltin 1987, 21).

Technicolor's new three-colour process, essentially an additive colouration process, provided an opportunity for Disney to differentiate his animation from that of his competitors. Additionally, for Technicolor, a partnership with Disney provided a way to reverse the opinions of cinemagoers that had criticized the colours of earlier processes as 'artificial and distracting' (Neupert 1994, 110). With Hollywood still unsure as to 'precisely what it wanted from – and indeed whether it wanted or even *needed* to pursue – colour cinematography' (Telotte 2008, 44), due to doubts of the process's ability to create a natural image, Technicolor saw animation as the perfect medium to showcase its refined technology. While providing an exaggeration of the real, Disney's cartoons, in particular, provided pleasure through 'their ability to *approach* the natural world, to make their constructions suggest a recognisable reality, while also offering an interpretation of that reality' (Telotte 2008, 47). In Disney, 'Technicolor had a client that not only was sympathetic to innovation, but also had a product, the animated cartoon, that might show its technology to maximum effect' (Telotte 2008, 47).

Knowing that the three-colour process would immediately become a highly desired commodity within animation, Disney looked for a way to safeguard his investment (the process added an additional $10,000 per cartoon in production costs). Shrewdly, he negotiated an exclusive deal with Technicolor that prevented competing animation studios from using it, most notably Iwerks, who had planned 'a series of sound and colour cartoons with classical music . . . to compete directly with "Silly Symphonies"' (Eliot 2003, 62). Crucially, having technological exclusivity within the animation industry for a short period of time allowed Disney to become the industry's principal studio. The colour cartoons released, namely the *Silly Symphonies*, maintained a mesmeric stranglehold on American audiences, due as much to their work-ethic positivity (typified by Practical Pig in *Three Little Pigs* [1933] and the benevolently industrious ants of *The Grasshopper and the Ants* [1934]) at a time of economic depression, as to their artistic sophistication.

Multiplane

This process of developing existing technologies to a fractionally higher standard, or capitalizing on emergent ones and then using them to enhance the Studio's animation and reputation, is not limited to the sound and colour breakthroughs of the late 1920s and early 1930s. During the 1930s, Disney's increasing drive for ever more realistic animation led to a number of in-house developments, with the most notable being the multiplane camera – an apparatus used to create three-dimensionality within an animated image. To achieve this depth:

the animation, background paintings, and overlay paintings might be on as many as six different levels, with the backgrounds and overlays painted on sheets of glass mounted a foot or more apart. As the camera trucked forward, different levels would come in and out of focus, as if they had been photographed by a live-action camera. (Barrier 1999, 249)

However, despite Amy M. Davis citing 'the invention by a Disney studio employee of the multi-plane camera' (2006, 40) as an example of the Studio's inventiveness, the Studio's multiplane apparatus was, in reality, purely the latest step in the evolution of depth in animation. Furthermore, the 1938 patent filed for this camera, coupled with its industrial notoriety, frequently obscures the developmental history of this device pre-Disney.

The Adventures of Prince Achmed (1926), the earliest surviving example of feature-length animation, while offering an animated extension of the contemporary German expressionist aesthetic, also pioneered 'an early form of the multi-plane camera, separating foregrounds and backgrounds into layers to give a 3-D effect' (Beck 2005, 4). Lotte Reiniger achieved this through a silhouette process of animation, not dissimilar in appearance to Asian shadow puppetry, whereby cardboard cut-outs and sheets of lead were filmed at differing distances from the camera, thus creating an illusion of depth. Moreover, as Esther Leslie notes, 'variegated tones suggested an illusion of distance', with Reiniger focused on creating 'a world of conventional physical laws. Gravity and perspective ruled' (2004, 49–50).

A decade later, the 'Stereoptical' process, developed by the Fleischer Studios, utilized three-dimensional backgrounds to create depth. These sets, 'mounted on a huge turntable that weighed two and half tons' (Fleischer 2005, 84), required detailed preparation for each sequence. The resulting animation exhibits a particularly believable sense of depth, an example of which can be seen (00:01:43–00:02:08) in the *Popeye* short *Lil Swee' Pea* (1936). During these 'Stereoptical' sequences, the background is constructed in such a way as to allow details at different distances from the camera to move at different speeds. The patent makes reference to this key feature, stating: 'a film made in this manner, when projected, will depict the various objects of the background moving in proper perspective and at proper relative speeds' (Fleischer 1936, 3).

While the aforementioned processes rely on the construction of 'sets' (lead planes in Reiniger's case) to establish a sense of depth, Disney's multiplane camera, paradoxically, makes exclusive use of multiple planes of flat animation to create an illusion of depth. However, Disney was not the first to create depth in such a way. Iwerks, ever the master technician, pioneered such a camera in 1934 in an attempt to develop the animation of his fledgling studio (Telotte 2006, 10). One major difference between the Iwerks and Disney multiplane cameras, however, was that Iwerks's design arranged the planes horizontally, while Disney's camera worked vertically. Additionally, Iwerks's 'home-brew' camera – built 'out of parts of an old Chevy that he had bought for $350' (Iwerks and Kenworthy 2001, 130) – cost far less to develop than Disney's multiplane camera.

The horizontal design of Iwerks's camera meant that it was able to accommodate stop-motion animation as well as cel animation. While the effectiveness of Iwerks's multiplane camera can be seen in the 1934 *Comicolor Classics* (1933–36), *The Headless Horseman* and *Don Quixote*, no example of stop-motion animation using the studio's multiplane camera exists. Despite the Iwerks Studios's starting production on *The Toy Parade*, which utilized both the multiplane camera and stop-motion animation, it was 'never released using the new multiplane technology' (Iwerks and Kenworthy 2001, 130) – a reflection, perhaps, of the studio's specialization in cel animation and unfamiliarity with the labour intensive nature of stop-motion animation, rather than of the quality of the unseen short. Leslie Iwerks and John Kenworthy observe that, after spending days incrementally repositioning wooden soldiers so that they could parade 'tediously across the screen', animator Ralph Somerville was 'ready to return to cel animation and the relative normalcy of the Comicolor Classics' (2001, 130–1).

Although both the Fleischer Studios and the Iwerks Studios made significant contributions to the development of animated depth-of-field, William E. Garity, the chief technician at Disney, did make several noteworthy refinements to the multiplane camera. The most important of these was the decision to introduce more planes into the camera's design – all of which were capable of containing a field of animation. Consequently, Garity's camera provided a greater level of control over movement and focus than the earlier depth-of-field generating technologies. However, the number of planes featured in Garity's design, in addition to facilitating increasingly sophisticated animated depth, also introduced lighting problems. As each plane was lit individually, the lighting needed to be consistent on each level, which, because the bulbs started blue but became red as they deteriorated, proved challenging. To control this, each bulb's life span was recorded, allowing for them to be removed before they reddened (Thomas 1997, 72). Furthermore, David Hand, in a production meeting during *Snow White*'s development, drew the animators' attention to the fact that the more planes (cels) of animation that they used, the less light was able to illuminate the scene's background. Hand comments: 'On the multiplane camera only four cels cut down the light by 56%. So, all you animators try to confine yourself – if you can't do it yourself . . . put it on the scene for the inkers to cut down the cels and to get more light on the background' (Williams 1987c). While Garity's multiplane did offer new cinematographic possibilities, it was, as we have seen, essentially just the latest iteration in the device's evolution.

Conclusion

The technological advances discussed above dramatically increased the cost of cartoon production for Disney. In order to maintain the development of these technologies within his Studio, Disney turned to feature-length animation as a way of generating enough profit to stay afloat in a turbulent economy and competitive market. The success of *Snow White* quickly identified feature animation as a significant profit-making endeavour.

During the protracted development of *Fantasia*, Disney remarked, '[w]e have to keep those things rolling out. If we don't get a feature out every so often, we're going to go broke. They must come out' (Solomon 1995, 37–8). In order for the Studio to develop beyond a purveyor of novelty attractions, the full commercial potential of the animated feature needed to be exploited. While merchandizing had been part of the Studio since the start of the 1930s, with the release of *Snow White* it reached new heights; as 'early as 1936, the company had granted over 70 licenses to various companies to produce a wide range of items, including clothing, food, toys, books' (Wasko 2001, 14).

When viewed in this context, *Snow White*'s divergences from the Grimms' fairy tale (Snow-Drop) begin to make commercial sense. This is most obvious in the way Disney develops the seven dwarfs. The dwarfs, homogenous in the Grimms' original, featuring primarily to remedy Snow White's ailments and offer guidance, are easily distinguished through names and matching traits in the Disney film. Moreover, the 'cute' representation of the dwarfs, coupled with their carefully chosen names, turns the sidekicks into exceptionally marketable commodities; a dwarf named Deafy – part of *Snow White*'s development up until 1936 (Williams 1987d) – evolved into Sneezy because the Studio didn't want names that suggested a 'serious physical affliction' (Barrier 1999, 201). A quick search of the Disney website will reveal the lasting appeal of these characters, as a plethora of products continue to incorporate the seven dwarfs. Today, the 'worldwide proliferation of merchandise is one of the key features of the Disney empire' (Wasko 2001, 48). It is with the animated feature that Disney made perhaps his greatest contribution to the animated medium. Furthermore, with his initial animated features, Disney established a formal blueprint that would inform not only the vast majority of the Studio's subsequent releases, but also many animated features produced by studios other than Disney.

Part 2

Early and Middle Disney
Feature Animation

Chapter 3

Disney-Formalism

Introduction

The phrase 'Classic Disney' has evolved in recent years, developing from a seemingly straightforward term featured in numerous discussions of Disney, to one which lacks the specificity required to support critical engagement with the Studio's animated features. In response, the term 'Disney-Formalism' will be developed in this chapter, and throughout this book, as an alternative to 'Classic Disney', and will relate directly to the formation, and continuation, of the aesthetic style forged in the films *Snow White and the Seven Dwarfs* (1937), *Pinocchio* (1940), *Dumbo* (1941) and *Bambi* (1942).[1]

These films, that 'established the creative high-watermark of the early Disney Studio' (Watts 1997, 83), form the basis of Disney-Formalist animation. During this eight-year period (from the commencement of *Snow White* to the release of *Bambi*) Disney made his most telling, and original, contributions to animation. Fundamentally, the Disney-Formalist ideology prioritized artistic sophistication, 'realism' in characters and contexts, and, above all, believability. However, before we discuss how the aforementioned films helped establish this artistic model, it will be useful to first consider what exactly the phrase 'Classic Disney' has come to denote.

Unpacking 'Classic Disney'

In early usage, 'Classic Disney' was used to periodize animation in a qualitative sense. For example, Leonard Maltin, writing in 1973, about a

---

[1] The use of Formalism in Disney-Formalism refers to the emphasis placed on a particular aesthetic form, and the determining industrial processes which underpin it. The name Disney-Formalism is not intended as a reference to Russian Formalism and the style of formalism associated with that literary movement.

passage of animation and live action in *Bedknobs and Broomsticks* (1971), states that the sequence is 'quite different from that of the recent Disney features . . . The drawing is funnier to begin with, and the character styling more in the classic Disney mould than in the rough-line method used in recent feature films' (1973, 262). The denotation of the term expanded drastically during the 1980s. In 1983, writing for *American Cinematographer*, Art Shifrin used the phrase 'Classic Disney' to make an industrial comparison. Although Shifrin's article is concerned with the study of Thomas Edison's Kinetophone and issues of fidelity surrounding copies of the device's original recordings, he turns to animation to help elaborate his argument:

> The problem that is inherent to these films is that each frame was exposed for at least 50% longer than a comparable frame of film would be shot today. Because of that, the nuances, especially of lip movement are diminished. Therefore some kinds of movement resemble those in cheap animations which have fewer cels per unit of time than say, a Classic Disney production. (1983, 125)

Clearly a shift in emphasis can be seen between Maltin's reference and Shifrin's; whereas Maltin refers to a classic period, Shifrin is less interested in historicizing the animation, instead alluding to 'Classic Disney' production methods and the Studio's commitment to quality.

With the emergence of the home video market, Disney appropriated the term 'Classic' for the VHS debuts of its animated features. First to be released under 'The Classics' label was *Robin Hood* (1973), which went into distribution in 1984. During the 1980s, Disney used this series as a way to recommodify its existing animated features. Frederick Wasser writes:

> Although the classic movies were designed and produced long before video, the sell-through versions of these old animations had become critical in pushing Disney to the top rank of the video market. The executives decided to maximise the shelf life of the classics by offering the videotapes for sale for limited periods, maximising sales without flooding the market with tapes that would circulate indefinitely. The challenge was to avoid exhausting the old library of classic animation and to build further. [Jeffery] Katzenberg *decided to make new Disney classics* to replenish the old ones. (2001, 165, emphasis added)

Although Disney initially conceived 'The Classics' series as a means of extending the commercial lives of their most popular and successful animated features, a number of live-action–animation hybrids have since been released under 'The Classics' banner (such as *Mary Poppins* [1964] and *Bedknobs and Broomsticks*). Due to the success of 'The Classics' series, Disney's theatrically released animated features have been reissued in several other guises, such as 'Gold Classics', the 'Masterpiece' collection and the 'Platinum' range.

Perhaps the most common association that has developed around the term 'Classic Disney' concerns the use, and co-option, of fairy tale narratives. As Maureen Furniss notes, 'many of the studio's features . . . have been based on well-known stories: folktales (also called fairytales), fables, myths, and legends' (2007, 114). This is hardly surprising, given the perceived homogeneity of Disney feature animation and the universality of fairy tale narratives (see Vladimir Propp's *Morphology of the Folktale* [1928] and Joseph Campbell's *The Hero with a Thousand Faces* [1949]). Moreover, the legion of identikit orphans (both human and animal) that dominate the Studio's animation frequently fulfil what Campbell terms the 'nuclear unit of the monomyth' (1993, 30), in which a hero 'ventures forth from the world of common day into a region of supernatural wonder: fabulous forces are there encountered and a decisive victory is won: the hero comes back from this . . . adventure with [newfound] power' (1993, 30). On a superficial level, this 'maturation' narrative can be seen throughout much of Disney's oeuvre.

For Jack Zipes, what is most worrying about the Studio's use of the fairy tale is the ability of Disney's signature to obfuscate such names as Charles Perrault, the Brothers Grimm, Hans Christian Anderson and Carlo Collodi. Zipes argues: 'If children or adults think of the great classical fairy tales today, be it *Snow White, Sleeping Beauty* [1959], or *Cinderella* (1950), they will think Walt Disney. Their first and perhaps lasting impressions of these tales and others will have emanated from a Disney film, book, or artefact' (1996, 21). However, despite Disney's success at co-opting fairy tale narratives and the recurrence of fairy tale iconography within the Studio's animation, it is incorrect to assert that this is true of every Disney animated feature. The existence of films such as *Dumbo, Bambi* and *Make Mine Music* (1946) problematize the utilization of 'Classic Disney' as a way of identifying the fairy tale's dominance within Disney animation.

In recent years, the complexity of 'Classic Disney' as a term has been discussed in a number of critical studies. Mark Philips, in a study of how

Disney is received, observes that certain spectators actively distinguish 'between "classic Disney" and current Disney' (2001, 48) – a distinction which is based on an understanding of the Studio's shift from being primarily a producer of animated entertainment to the globally diversified business it is today. Janet Wasko, in her study *Understanding Disney* (2001), provides a survey of the many constituent elements that help shape 'Classic Disney'. Wasko writes:

> It is possible . . . to identify something called 'Classic Disney,' which refers to the company's animated films, cartoons, and some live-action films, plus the stable of characters which emerge from these productions, as well as the consistent set of themes and values that generally represent 'Disney' to the general public and critical analysis. (2001, 110)

While attempting to provide the broadest possible study, Wasko still concedes that 'there are exceptions and variations, as not all of the characteristics have been included in every product or text' (2001, 113). These attempts to define 'Classic Disney', which work within the existing nomenclature, do little more than highlight the need for a critical alternative to the term.

Snow White and the Foundations of Disney-Formalism

Immediately after announcing his arrival with the release of *Steamboat Willie*, Disney had to contend with the difficult conditions of economic depression. In the United States, the Great Depression lasted roughly twelve years, spanning from 1929 to 1941. Thomas Emerson Hall and J. David Ferguson note that the worst of the Depression

> was during the first three and a half years when virtually every single indicator of economic prosperity reflected the disaster. The falling levels of economic output resulted in widespread human misery, the extent of which is measured by the rising level of unemployment, increased poverty, and high rates of default on debt by both firms and households. (1998, 1)

However, Disney's escapist and aspirational cartoons helped develop the Studio into a profitable business. Steven Watts writes, 'although not as big as enterprises such as Universal, Columbia, and RKO, Disney's independent operation had clearly entered the realm of big business by the early 1930s' (1997, 66). In financial terms, 'each [cartoon] cost about $50,000 to make, and each had an expected profit of roughly $120,000, minus distribution costs, in its first two years of release' (Watts 1997, 66).

Despite such figures, much of the money Disney made was immediately reinvested in a continual attempt to raise the quality of the Studio's animation, garnering the Studio a variety of awards; however, this also meant that the production of new cartoons proved a financial balancing act. This was not the conventional practice for animation studios at that time, as not every studio chose to walk the economic tightrope. Richard Fleischer, son of Max Fleischer, notes:

> Max never talked about it much, but Disney's constant winning of awards, for the beauty and graceful animation of his cartoons, rankled. It was well known in the industry that, because of the award-winning quality of Disney's cartoons, they were too expensive, and the Disney Company was frequently close to going broke. I once asked my father if he ever envied Disney's ability to cop so many accolades. His answer was straightforward and telling. 'Just remember one thing,' he said. 'You can't eat medals'. (2005, 73–4)

While the Fleischer Studios was content to develop conservatively during the time of economic downturn, Disney, buoyed by his Studio's profitability, sought to expand beyond short cartoons with the feature-length *Snow White*.

Snow White's success profoundly altered the Studio. Although the film generated unprecedented negative costs for an animation production, 'almost $1.5 million, just a little less than the Disney studio's total revenues in 1937' (Barrier 2008, 130), it enabled Disney to make much larger profits. In the year of *Snow White*'s release 'income was $1.565 million, including $1.187 million in film rentals. In 1938, in the first nine months alone, total income was . . . $4.346 million' (Barrier 2008, 131). This dramatic rise in income can be partially attributed to the Studio's growing range of merchandise, which, as noted in the previous chapter, included 'clothing, food, toys, books, phonograph records, and sheet music' (Wasko 2001, 14). Ultimately, the financial and critical success of *Snow White*, coupled with the comparative failure of *Fantasia* (1940), led to the former becoming an aesthetic blueprint for much of the

Disney-Formalist period. The artistic paradigm promoted by *Snow White* has since become known as 'hyperrealism'.

Hyperrealism, as a term, is not unique to animation. However, Disney – or more specifically, Disneyland – does provide the means by which theorists such as Umberto Eco and Jean Baudrillard engage with the concept. Both Eco and Baudrillard, using Disneyland as an example, utilize the term to debate issues of cultural reproduction in the twentieth century:

> For Eco, Disneyland is the ultimate example of what he sees as an emergent postmodernist culture characterized by the 'fake' (others include waxwork museums and animatronic displays), whereas for Baudrillard our enjoyment of the theme park's emphasis on its own spectacular 'hyperreality' serves to distract us from the fact that the real world as a whole is now hyperreal: there is no real left to 'fake'. (Dovey et al. 2009, 138)

Although both Eco and Baudrillard problematize constructions of 'reality' in ways that are characteristic of postmodernism, within animation studies the term 'hyperrealism' has acquired different and more specific meanings.

Hyperrealism, as deployed in the works of animation theorist Paul Wells, has come to define a mode of animation which, despite the medium's obvious artifice, strives for 'realism'. It is this paradox – the attempt to represent reality in a medium predicated on artificiality – that makes hyperrealism such an appropriate term. Conventionalized during the Disney-Formalist period (as discussed below), the Studio's hyperrealism is frequently seen 'as the yardstick by which other kinds of animation may be measured for its relative degree of "realism"' (Wells 1998, 25). Although this 'realist' style is often taken to represent the work of the Studio *in toto*, this misrepresents a substantial proportion of the Studio's animation oeuvre. Much of Disney's early animation resisted the conventions of realism, and like the contemporary shorts such as *Felix the Cat* (1920–28) and *Out of the Inkwell* (1919–29), *Oswald the Rabbit* (1927–28), *Mickey Mouse* (1928–99) and the *Silly Symphonies* featured exaggerated squash-and-stretch physics and cartoonal metamorphosis. However, with the change to Disney-Formalist feature animation the pursuit of realism quickly became the overriding concern.

This desire is evident in a *Snow White* production meeting held in 1936. Taking the lead, and introducing a number of the concerns facing the animators, Hamilton Luske raises the issue of how Snow White's eyes are to be depicted. Conscious of the need to reconcile realism within the animated form, Luske observes: 'We see this girl with round eyes – just as round as we can make them. If we get too large eyes, like some of the comic strips, she gets into the Betty Boop type' (Williams 1987b). Furthermore, the emphasis on believability leads the animators present at this meeting to question how best to depict Snow White's mouth. Luske again takes the lead, arguing that if her mouth is not correctly animated, people might criticize it for not having 'enough form to it', before concluding: 'We have a mouth we have to put teeth in, etc., and still make it look realistic' (Williams 1987b).

The most significant element of Disney-Formalist hyperrealism is the lifelike movement – or motor function – of the animation, which reflects both the actual movements of live-action models and the skill of the animator. By employing a more studied variety of squash-and-stretch movement, from one drawing to the next, it quickly 'became the very essence of animation' (Thomas and Johnson 1995, 48). As Frank Thomas and Ollie Johnson note, squash-and-stretch had the potential to affect all aspects of animation: 'a smile was no longer a simple line spread across a face; it now defined the lips and their relation to the cheeks. Legs were no longer . . . rubber hoses; they swelled as they bent and stretched to long flexible shapes' (1995, 48).

In the case of Disney animation, 'filmed actions of humans and animals [were also] used in many ways . . . [leading] to some important discoveries' (Thomas and Johnson 1995, 319). In the Studio's early Disney-Formalist features, rather than simply follow a strategy of rotoscoping, a method employed by the Fleischer Studios in their *Betty Boop* (1932–39) series and in the feature-length *Gulliver's Travels* (1939), the Studio's animators used live action solely as a guide. Disney himself once remarked how useful filmed action could be when viewed frame by frame, stating: 'I used to see things there that I could never imagine' (Williams 1987a). In contrast to the Studio's preferred realism, strictly rotoscoped animation had a tendency to 'lose the illusion of life', because, as Thomas and Johnson argue, despite the accuracy in the movement provided by rotoscope, 'it was impossible to become emotionally involved with [the] . . . shadowy creature who was never a real inhabitant of our fantasy world' (1995, 323). This view, though, may reflect the remit of Thomas and Johnson's Hyperion edition: to make a claim for Disney animation as art, where the non-rotoscoped work of the Studio promotes 'the personal statement of an artist' (1995, 323) – a claim that is a little paradoxical given the Taylorist methods of produc-tion employed by the Studio. However, there is some basis to this claim, as Paul Ward has also argued that entirely rotoscoped 'animation often look[s] strange, eerie, or out of place' (2006, 233), a style which, in rela-tion to hyperrealism, would prove counterproductive. A key strength of the Disney animators, therefore, lay in their decision to 'use the Photo-stats only as a reference', after which subsequent 'animation picked up a crispness, a force, and a richness it never had before' (Thomas and Johnson 1995, 323).

The evolution of Disney-Formalist hyperrealism should not be thought of as a linear progression, however, but rather the sum, or reconciliation, of competing approaches. One such approach, emphasized by Disney during the development of Snow White as a character, was 'cuteness'. Zack Schwartz, an animator at Disney during the Studio's 'Golden Age', remarks: 'that word 'cute' used to drive me crazy, it was all over the stu-dio' (Frayling et al. 1997, 5). Such an emphasis may have reflected the realization that a completely realistic human figure could not be depicted using traditional 2-D hand animation, given that the medium constantly, and unavoidably, foregrounds its artifice. Wells writes:

> The construction of the 'body', even in the most determinedly hyper-realist animation (most specifically, Disney), is a complex issue, largely because animation has the capacity to resist 'realism' and the ortho-doxies of the physical world, redefining the body as a fluid and indes-tructible form. Compressing, disassembling, reassembling, adjusting to impossible environments and changing shape at the animator's will. (1996, 185)

Schwartz acknowledges the inherent paradox of using traditional 2-D animation to depict 'realistic' images, commenting: 'On the one hand Disney was highly appreciative of the fact that you had to caricature stuff to make it act. On the other hand the drive towards reality is always there too' (Frayling et al. 1997, 6). Ultimately, believability, rather than abso-lute realism, became the driving principle underpinning Disney's anima-tion during this period.

This stylistic specificity, which found a major platform with the release of *Snow White*, had a far-reaching effect on the surrounding animation industry. The Studio's closest competition at this time, the Fleischer Studios, saw 'a shift not just toward more Disney-like drawing, but also toward more Disney-like procedures' (Barrier 2008, 294). Michael Barrier discusses this change with reference to a scene in *Gulliver's Travels*: 'The sequence in which King Little of Lilliput and King Bombo of Blefuscu fall out was made to order for animation of the kind that emerged in *Snow White*: bring the kings to life, make their quarrel *real*, and the pretext for that quarrel could quickly become irrelevant' (2008, 295, emphasis added). From the outset, Disney's hyperrealism was a source of inspiration to those animators outside of the Studio seeking to generate a similar level of verisimilitude in their animation.

In addition to the insistence on realistic character movement, each cel was subject to post-compositional revision in an attempt to maximize the intrinsic visual realism of every frame. While men occupied the most senior positions within Disney's animating hierarchy – a status quo maintained by Disney's 'hunting [for] men' (Eliot 2003, 69) in standard job adverts – the inking-and-painting department had many female staff members. Marc Eliot asserts that jobs 'in the inking-and-painting department required little skill beyond being able to colour' (Eliot 2003, 29), but the women (and men) who worked in this division of the Studio had the privilege of seeing cels in their finished state. When viewing the finished *Snow White* cels, 'some of the women felt that the black hair looked *unnatural* and harsh, so they tried adding a wisp of drybrush in a lighter grey to soften the edge of her hair' (Thomas and Johnson 1995, 277, emphasis added). Furthermore, whereas the contemporaneous character 'Jenny Wren's cheeks were painted with circles of pink paint', resulting in a clown-like appearance, 'a more *natural* look' was achieved on Snow White, with a 'delicate tint of rouge, carefully rubbed on top of each cel' by ink-and-painting (Thomas and Johnson 1995, 276, emphasis added). In keeping with Disney's insistence on 'verisimilitude in . . . characters, contexts and narratives' (Wells 1998, 23), all planes of the animation hierarchy – including the women working in the inking-and-painting department – strived to achieve a naturalistic image by any means necessary. In doing so, the inkers and painters brought a previously unmatched level of femininity to the young protagonist.

Lastly, as a product of 'Disney's insistence on realism in *Snow White*'?, cartoonal metamorphosis, is, with the exception of the Queen's transformation into the Witch, largely absent. Wells defines cartoonal metamorphosis as the image's ability 'to literally change into another completely different image' through 'the evolution of the line' (1998, 69). It was exactly these characteristics that made Soviet filmmaker and theorist Sergei Eisenstein an unlikely fan of the Studio's work. For Eisenstein, the characters of Disney's early films, which 'could often be found dancing on musical notes, and . . . would often be metamorphosed into musical instruments – towels becoming piano rolls, tails turning into violins' (Canemaker 1994), were a 'plasmatic' revelation. Through 'plasmaticness' Eisenstein was referring to animation's 'rejection of once-and-forever allotted form, freedom from ossification, [and] the ability to dynamically assume any form' (1986, 5). This style of animation, Eisenstein argued, behaved 'like . . . primal protoplasm, not yet possessing a "stable" form' and was 'capable of . . . skipping along the rungs of the evolutionary ladder' (1986, 5). Eisenstein adds, to a 'social order with such a mercilessly standardized and mechanically measured existence . . . the sight of such "omnipotence" (that is, the ability to become "whatever you wish"), cannot but hold a sharp degree of attractiveness' (1986, 5). It is ironic, then, that the hyperrealist style of animation developed during the Disney-Formalist period, which has come to signify the Studio's work as a whole, is both standardized and mechanically measured, and has sacrificed the 'plasmaticness' of the early shorts and some of the 'Package features' for realism.

Pinocchio

Pinocchio saw Disney again strive to advance the sophistication of his Studio's animation. Maltin argues that, despite financial stresses, 'Disney refused to compromise with quality, and he was determined to incorporate into *Pinocchio* all the lessons he had learned during the production of *Snow White*' (1987, 58). This drive for perfection is reflected in the detailing of Jiminy Cricket. Senior animator Frank Thomas reveals that twenty-seven different colours were used for the Jiminy Cricket character: 'You can't even think of twenty-seven parts of him to paint, let alone different colours to paint them . . . But [Walt] wanted the thing to look real' (Watts 1997, 106).

While we have discussed the strategies employed at Disney to enhance the realism of their animation during the *production* of the animation cels, we have yet to consider how similar results were achieved through the profilmic *arrangement* of cels. We are, of course, referring to the Studio's use of the multiplane camera (see Chapter 2), which, by fixing cels at various distances from the lens, was able to simulate depth-of-field. Essentially, depth-of-field refers to the 'range of distances before the lens within which objects can be photographed in sharp focus' (Bordwell and Thompson 2001, 202). However, because not all the planes are in focus

FIGURES 3.1–3.7 (left to right) Establishing depth in *Pinocchio*

at any one time, and the camera has freedom to alter focus by transitioning between layers, this method of animating is closer to the live-action concept of deep space, where a live-action filmmaker stages 'action on several planes, *regardless of whether or not all of these planes are in focus*' (Bordwell and Thompson 2001, 202).

The following sequence, taken from *Pinocchio* (Figures 3.1–3.7), through which the camera shifts focus, demonstrates how multiple, simultaneously filmed planes of animation can establish a sense of depth within a composite image.

Starting in Figure 3.1, we see four identifiable planes of animation: the background (A), the middle ground (B), the foreground (C), and the white doves overlay (D). While the lateral motion occurring between Figures 3.1 and 3.2 does little to establish depth, the doves, sent into flight by the chiming bell, act as a focal point for the viewer as the perspective changes to a high angle shot. As the camera begins to 'track towards' (zoom into) the mountain village (Figure 3.3), the plane of animation containing the doves moves out of focus. Despite the re-centred action, the original four planes of animation are still employed; however, now the camera begins to move 'through' the planes, bringing the originally distant background (A) and middle ground (B) into sharp focus. This camera movement is essential in establishing a sense of depth. As the original foreground (C) moves out of shot, a further plane of animation (E) becomes visible behind it (Figure 3.3). With the village square revealed (Figures 3.4 and 3.5), a number of animated figures begin to cross the scene, reorientating the camera laterally, in much the same way as the doves in Figure 3.3. The camera, now centred on the newly revealed plane (E), begins to refocus, roaming deeper into the village, before coming to rest on Pinocchio's house (Figure 3.6); at this point there is a cut, providing a transition into a more conventionally animated sequence (Figure 3.7).

Disney once remarked, '*Pinocchio* might have lacked *Snow White*'s heart appeal, but technically and artistically it was superior' (Maltin 1987, 58). Central to this assessment is the intricate detailing of *Pinocchio* and the virtuosity with which the multiplane camera was used within the film; to produce the sequence described above, which lasts for less than a minute, cost Disney 'an estimated $45,000' (Solomon 1994, 59). However, the ongoing development of hyperrealism, clearly evident in *Pinocchio*, did not continue in a straightforward manner during the production of *Dumbo*.

Dumbo

Dumbo, the flying elephant, could be viewed as the clearest contradiction of Disney-Formalist hyperrealism. However, Dumbo's animated movements – when not airborne – reveal a careful study of live-action animal motor function. Interestingly, in an attempt to encourage this studied detail, 'Disney kept a small zoo in the studio so artists could draw from nature' (Schickel 1997, 180). Although, while animals were required to 'move like real animals . . . it was important that the complexity of this movement . . . be unnoticeable, a condition achieved through the dexterity of the artist's skills in drawing creatures' (Wells 1998, 23).

The memorable 'Pink Elephants on Parade' sequence, which diverges from the established conventions of Disney-Formalism, is less obviously reconcilable. In spite of Dumbo's alcohol drinking, which acts as a causal framing device legitimizing the sudden surreal transition, this sequence employs an aesthetic found very rarely in Disney feature animation as a whole, let alone that of the Disney-Formalist period. What we are presented with in this sequence is the animated form's fundamental *raison d'être*: the ability to conceive and show what pure live action can't, with the only limitation being the skill and imagination of the animator. Moreover, it signified a return to the plasmatic metamorphosis and exaggerated squash-and-stretch physicality of the early shorts.

Midway through the 'Pink Elephants' interlude, a bipedal figure composed of elephant heads marches towards the camera, and as it nears, its eyes mutate into pyramids. From between these pyramids a camel-elephant (or 'Camelephant') hybrid emerges; in addition to its fantastical pedigree it also displays a noticeable squash-and-stretch physicality. The 'Camelephant' then passes a pyramid that morphs into a snake charmer; the music the snake charmer plays causes the 'Camelephant' to metamorphosize into a snake. The snake then transforms into an elephant woman with humanoid appearance; as she performs a veil dance her body regresses into a simple ball shape – a visual reference to the circular principles of early 'rubber-hose animation'. This constant switching of form, which occurs throughout the 'Pink Elephants' interlude, lends the sequence a distinctly surrealist quality, which contrasts dramatically with conventional hyperrealist aesthetics of Disney-Formalism.

Mark Langer points to regionalism as a way of explaining the disparate nature of *Dumbo*. Langer identifies two schools of animation, situated on opposing coasts of the United States, which influenced the film's look: 'New York Style' (NYS) and 'West Coast Style' (WCS). The NYS, of which the 'Pink Elephants' sequence is emblematic, was 'predominantly a "cartoony" style, where the artificiality of the characters and their drawn nature were emphasized through design, movement, and dialogue' (Langer 1990, 308). This quality was achieved by using ' "rubber animation" in which both animate and inanimate objects moved with bouncy flexibility as if they were made of rubber. Objects took on the function or characteristics of other things, emphasising mutability and metamorphosis' (Langer 1990, 308). Contrastingly, Langer notes that the WCS 'incorporated a number of strategies, primary of which was the emulation of the narrative and stylistic codes of classical cinema' (1990, 306). Additionally, the WCS defined by Langer sought to create 'coherent screen personalities' and replicate 'lifelike movement' (1990, 306). While Langer's WCS relates to the principles of hyperrealism, his definition also has a broader scope, encompassing short animation as well as animation from studios other than Disney.

Having outlined these contrasting styles, Langer recasts Dumbo's predicament as a struggle between the principles of the NYS and the WCS. Langer sees the NYS 'Pink Elephants' as identifying a metamorphic solution to the problems faced by Dumbo in the dominant WCS portion of the film. In his conclusion, Langer also highlights the parallel, extrafilmic struggle between the two styles that was occurring at the time of the film's production and release: 'The New York solution presented by the 'Pink Elephants' is normalised by the West Coast ending . . . *Dumbo*'s conclusion is not only a celebration of the typical Disney restoration of family and prosperity . . . it also celebrates the triumph of the West coast style' (1990, 318). In fact, it is on a similarly industrial level that the 'Pink Elephants' sequence is best understood.

Langer identifies three animators, Dick Huemer, Joe Grant and Norman Ferguson, all of whom started their careers in New York, who were largely responsible for the 'Pink Elephants' sequence. Langer clearly implies that it is *because of* these animators that the NYS emerges within the film, arguing that Huemer and Grant 'rewrote the story', thus facilitating Ferguson's 'pivotal "Pink Elephants" sequence' (1990, 310). However, Langer does not make any reference to Ferguson's earlier roles at Disney, such as 'supervising animator for *Snow White*, [where] he oversaw a number of sequences and personally drew the evil witch, the first of the great Disney villains' (Watts 1997, 132). Additionally, Disney may have afforded Ferguson more artistic freedom than other animators in his staff, because, in the words of Huemer: 'Fergy . . . was it. Not only the best at Disney's but consequently the best in the world' (Watts 1997, 132). However, as *Bambi* testifies, the aesthetic hybridity developed in *Dumbo* was to be short-lived.

Bambi

Bambi represents the hyperrealist peak of the Studio's Disney-Formalist animation, building on the previous animated features in a number of ways. Its development of existing practices is immediately visible in the film's opening multiplane sequence, which, at a length of one minute thirty-two seconds, runs fifty-one seconds longer than the *Pinocchio* multiplane discussed above. In addition, *Bambi*'s multiplane also features a dynamic shift in tracking speed between 00:02:36–00:02:47. While this multiplane sequence confirms the Studio's perfection of the mechanical aspects of Disney-Formalist animation, a similar degree of sophistication is evident in *Bambi*'s post-production special effects work.

Bambi's 'Little April Showers' sequence is one of the most effects-heavy sequences in Disney's animation oeuvre, presenting a visually striking depiction of a springtime downpour. Ub Iwerks offers the following explanation of how the Studio's effects animators achieved this: 'Falling water is photographed at night with a spotlight playing on it. The film is then put in a camera and enlarged prints made. Cartoon rain is added and the splatters are accentuated. The effect is much more lifelike than pen-and-ink rain, yet retains characteristics of animation' (Iwerks and Kenworthy 2001, 155–6). Furthermore, to retain the translucent quality of shallow water, the rippling rings at the sequence's conclusion 'were painted in lacquer on the cels, with no inked outline' (Thomas and Johnson 1995, 262). This artistic resourcefulness, fundamental in endowing *Bambi* with visual believability, is mirrored in the animator's depiction of the film's animals.

Despite Disney's desire for the animals to look as realistic as possible, achieving this was not always a smooth process. Solomon notes how 'the antlers of the majestic Prince of the Forest and the adult Bambi presented special difficulties. None of the artists could keep them in perspective and maintain their volume' (1994, 128). Furthermore, in pencil tests, the antlers 'looked rubbery and seemed to wobble' (Solomon 1994, 128). A solution, as Thomas and Johnson reveal, was reached by 'tracing a plaster model that could be turned in any direction to match the animator's drawing' (1995, 339).

During the production of *Bambi*, Disney made arrangements for real deer to be kept 'on the lot as models for the animators' (Finch 1995b, 209). As a product of the animators' proximity to real deer and Disney's insistence on a balance between realism and believability, the eye animation in *Bambi* reached a new level of sophistication. Thomas and Johnson write:

> Compared to Mickey or the dwarfs, the Bambi eyes appear to be very realistic. They are caricatures of a real deer's eyes rather than being cartoon eyes. We had the suggestion of a tear duct and had a carefully drawn upper eyelid with a thickness to it that fits over the eyeball. The pupil with the dark centre and the highlight made the eye the most detailed we had ever drawn. Most audiences would have been hard pressed to tell that a real deer's eye was any different. (1995, 448–9)

Despite the obvious detail in *Bambi*'s eye animation (Figure 3.8), Thomas and Johnson's assertion that they would be indistinguishable from a real deer's eyes remains a little hyperbolic.

FIGURE 3.8   Towards realism: animating Bambi's eyes

However, to fully appreciate how far Disney's animators moved away from the cartoon principles of the Studio's earlier shorts, it is worth detailing the contribution of Rico Lebrun during the film's preproduction. In order to best learn and understand about an animal, Lebrun believed it was important to physically interact with it. After coming into possession of 'the carcass of a very young fawn, no more than two days old', Lebrun arranged a series of evening classes in which he planned 'to remove the outer layers, a little each night . . . [revealing] all the intricate workings right down to the skeleton' (Thomas and Johnson 1995, 339). Thomas and Johnson recall how

> Rico removed the skin – so we could examine the muscles and the tendons and the remarkable engineering principles revealed in this wonder of nature. Unfortunately, each time he contracted or extended any part of the cadaver a rich aroma was pumped into the air. He called to us, 'Hey, fellas, get in here close where you can see what this thing is doing.' We answered warmly, 'Oh, we can see just fine from back here!' In spite of this unique opportunity to gain vast knowledge, attendance to those evening classes began to fall off. (1995, 339–41)

As a result of these various strategies, the animal physiology of Bambi – and the other deer – contrasts starkly with that of earlier Disney animals, such as Mickey Mouse, Donald Duck and even Dumbo.

In Disney's mind, *Bambi* represented the culmination of his Disney-Formalist aspirations, although, for others, the film marked the end of an era. Eisenstein, who had responded enthusiastically to Disney's shorts, sees *Bambi* as a 'shift towards ecstasy – serious, eternal' (1986, 63). The lyricism of *Bambi*, to which Eisenstein alludes, is also noted by Finch, who sees it separating '*Bambi* from all other Disney movies' (1995b, 207). While Eisenstein is not overtly critical of this shift in Disney's animation, disappointment can be detected in his esoteric evaluation of both the film and Disney's evolution:

> [T]he theme of *Bambi* is the circle of life – *the repeating circles of lives*. No longer the sophisticated smile of the twentieth century towards totems. But a return to pure totemism and a *Rück-Ruck* [reverse shift] towards evolutionary prehistory. A humanised deer, or rather, *Rückgänglich* [conversely] – a 're-deerised' human. *Bambi* crowns, of course, the whole study on Disney. Separately, there's still *Fantasia* as an experiment in the realisation of *synthesis* through *syncretism*.

The greatness of Disney, as the purest example of the application of the method of art in its very purest form. (1986, 63)

Bambi, for Eisenstein, marks a decisive rejection, on Disney's part, of the plasmatic potential of animation. Furthermore, his identification of *Fantasia* as the purest example of animation's ability to reconcile what might otherwise be disparate art forms (consider the abstract 'Toccata and Fugue in D Minor' introduction and the mythological visuals that accompany Beethoven's 'Pastoral Symphony'), which he also sees as the 'greatness of Disney', can be seen as a further admonishment of *Bambi*'s aesthetic orthodoxy.

In pursuing and reaching the limits of hyperrealist animation, Disney became the most visible studio in American animation, and, as Wells writes, 'it might properly be argued that all cartoon animation that follows the Disney output is a *reaction* to Disney, aesthetically, technically, and ideologically' (2002a, 45). Moreover, in that sense, much postwar 'American animation is effectively a history of responses to Disney's usurpation of the form in the period between 1933 and 1941' (Wells 2002a, 45).

Conclusion

Ultimately, the production of such highly detailed features became financially unviable. *Bambi*, the pinnacle of Disney-Formalism, took six years to complete, and did not generate the profits Disney anticipated, which was partly the result of the fact that World War II drastically reduced Disney's overseas markets. Additionally, in the final years of the war effort, Disney agreed to make a number of propagandist animations for the army air corps and the navy. Although this work helped keep the Studio solvent at such a challenging time, 'Disney did not enjoy working with many of the military officers and government officials who had to pass on his films' (Barrier 2008, 185). Subsequently, Disney spent the remainder of the 1940s rebuilding a stable financial base, achieving this by relying heavily on the 'Package' features *Saludos Amigos* (1942), *The Three Caballeros* (1944), *Make Mine Music* (1946), *Fun and Fancy Free* (1947), *Melody Time* (1948) and *The Adventures of Ichabod and Mr. Toad* (1949).

Disney-Formalist filmmaking, therefore, was established during a very brief period of Disney's early history, with the films *Snow White*, *Pinocchio*,

Dumbo and *Bambi*. Since then, however, numerous films have drawn upon the aesthetic traditions of Disney-Formalism, including the Disney Renaissance features and *The Princess and the Frog* (2009) – all of which will be discussed later in this book. Furthermore, non-Disney films such as *An American Tail* (1986), *Anastasia* (1997), *Quest For Camelot* (1998), *The Land Before Time* (1988), *The Magic Riddle* (1991) and *The Swan Princess* (1994) also reveal the influence of this Disney-Formalist tradition. Although a discussion of these films as examples of 'Classic Disney' filmmaking could result in confusion, seeing them as either an extension of hyperrealism or as paying homage to Disney-Formalist filmmaking provides an opportunity for a more focused engagement with the artistic motivations of each film. Therefore, terms such as hyperrealism and Disney-Formalism reduce, if not remove, the need to use the now over-determined phrase 'Classic Disney'. In fact, the need for greater specificity when dissecting Disney's animation oeuvre becomes immediately apparent when interpreting the works that follow immediately after the Disney-Formalist period.

Chapter 4

Destino

Introduction

Although Disney has a very definite identity, it is debatable whether this self-image rests comfortably within the Studio's collective consciousness. Over the past seventy years, dating from the release of *Snow White* (1937) and the foundation of Disney-Formalism, the Studio has acquired a reputation for consistent mainstream animation excellence. However, while this excellence has guaranteed that the Disney name features on numerous Academy Awards, it often excludes the Studio from more 'serious' artistic acclaim. One way Disney himself sought to ratify this was to invite the iconoclastic Salvador Dalí to the Burbank studios in 1946. Disney's proposition was simple – they would work together to produce a short surrealist animation. In 2003, the results of this collaboration were released as a short entitled *Destino*.

Destino, while not a feature-length animation, requires and deserves discussion. Regardless of the fact that it was initially conceived as a chapter for a package feature, a feature that never made it into production, *Destino* is arguably the most significant project started by Disney during the 1940s. In extant accounts of Disney animation, *Destino*'s place within this period of the Studio's history is frequently obfuscated by discussions of union unrest or package feature mediocrity. Competing with this established master narrative, which prioritizes Disney's withdrawal to a position of single-minded autocracy and which depicts the Studio floundering creatively during and after World War II (stunted by a stint as US military hired-hand), it is easy to see how the ambitious, collaborative, imaginative, and most importantly, complex *Destino* fails to occupy a larger part in the Disney narrative. Having taken almost sixty years to complete, *Destino* serves as a testament to the Studio's continued highbrow aspirations. Given its significance, and the lack of study devoted to it, this chapter examines the details of *Destino*'s conception, production and completion, and, in light of its limited exhibition, also provides a critical review of the short.

existed between the Dalí estate and the Studio, put in place by the original collaborators, which stipulated that the original Dalí artwork in the Disney archive would only become the property of the Studio upon the completion of *Destino*.

The completion of *Destino* was hindered by the unorganized, and in parts cryptic, condition of surviving material. Interpreting these enigmatic artefacts into one coherent sequence (a Disney requisite) was made considerably more difficult given that Dalí had always maintained, with regard to *Destino*, 'if you understand this, then I've failed' (Desowitz 2003a). Ultimately, direction of the project was assigned to French animator Dominique Monfery, with Baker Bloodworth installed in the role of producer. Of utmost importance to the Studio, after securing the rights to Dalí's *Destino* artwork, was ensuring that the short film matched Disney's original intentions: that it should enhance the profile of the Studio in the discerning eyes of the art community. In an attempt to guarantee this reception, the Studio limited *Destino*'s exhibition to elite film festivals during 2003, select major film events (making its debut at Cannes prior to garnering a nomination at the 76th Academy Awards), and restricted gallery exhibition. However, Disney's custodian role in the assemblage and exhibition of *Destino* paints only half the picture.

Surrealism and the Dalínian Politick

By opening the Burbank studio's doors to Dalí, Disney not only brought in-house one of the twentieth century's great eccentrics, he also effectively extended an invitation to the world of surrealism in the hope that it might earn the Studio highbrow acknowledgement. In 1946, Dalí's name would have connoted a particularly eccentric vision of surrealism, in light of the artist's association with works such as *The Lobster Telephone* (1936), *The Face of Mae West* (1934–35), *The Persistence of Memory* (1931), *The Great Masturbator* (1929) and the barbarous eyeball assault featured in *Un Chien Andalou* (1929). This Dalínian nexus is revealing for several reasons. First, it represents a very definite time period, from 1929 to 1936, during which Dalí, in surrealist eyes, attained a politico-artistic zenith. (It is crucial to note that Dalí's self-evident craftsmanship fiercely resists such categorization; one need only consider *The Chair* [1975] to see an example of his skill and experimentation in the twilight of his career.) Secondly, they adhere to the principles of André Breton's first surrealist manifesto, most notably in their consistent visual challenges to our means of interpretation. A key aspect of surrealism, according to Breton, was 'psychic automatism in its pure state, by which one proposes to express – verbally, by means of the written word, or in any other means – the actual functioning of thought. Dictated by thought, in the absence of any control exercised by reason, exempt from any aesthetic or moral concern' (1969, 26). Thirdly, the aforementioned works embody and anticipate many important themes of Dalí's life work, ranging from images such as the fetishized telephone, the limp watch, the female form and connoted meaning revolving around a psycho-sexual liberation. This artistic dynamism, coupled with his contemporary live-action vogue, would have attracted the culturally ambitious Disney to the prospect of collaborating with the Spanish surrealist. Surrealism, however, as 'one of the most extraordinary artistic and intellectual movements of the twentieth century' (Serota 2001, 7), represents a clear binary to the Disney ethos of representational conservatism; a conservative ideology that has impacted on numerous aspects of American animation, and which has helped foster a 'normative condition of animation substantially created by Disney' (Wells 2002b, 88).

Motivated by the writings of Sigmund Freud on the subject of the human psyche, specifically his theories regarding the latency of ideas 'before being made conscious' (1950, 12), surrealism became a widely recognized movement with the dissemination of Breton's first 'Manifesto of Surrealism'. A key Freudianism for Breton was the assertion that the 'ego represents what we call reason and sanity, in contrast to the id which contains passions' (1950, 30). This insight moved Breton to declare that

> The imagination is perhaps on the point of reclaiming its rights. If the depths of our mind harbour strange forces capable of increasing those of the surface, or of successfully contending with them, then it is all in our interest to canalise them, to canalise them first in order to submit them later, if necessary, to the control of reason. (1969, 10).

This argument that surrealism can be a tool for mass change, allowing us to look into 'our' minds, because it is in 'our' interests to do so, provides an early example of how Breton's and Dalí's conceptions of surrealism differ. Whereas Breton concerned himself with affecting wider change, Dalí's motivations were more personal.

Regardless, Dalí *was* an important figure within the movement. In fact, 'the rise to fame of Surrealism synchronized with the dazzling success of Salvador Dalí, one of the latest comers and most sensational of its exponents' (Waldberg 1962, 89). Moreover, Dalí's conception of what he termed the paranoiac-critical method confirmed his importance among the surrealists. Dalí defined the paranoiac-critical as a '*spontaneous method of irrational knowledge based on the interpretative-critical association of delirium phenomena*' (Bosquet 2003, 61). To which Breton subsequently suggested that the method's appeal revolved around Dalí's own strength 'to participate in these events as actor and spectator simultaneously, that he . . . succeeded in establishing himself both as judge of and party to the action instituted by pleasure against reality' (1972, 133). Breton was so impressed with Dalí's paranoiac-critical process that he praised it as 'an instrument of primary importance . . . capable of being applied with equal success to painting, poetry, the cinema, to the construction of typical surrealist objects, to fashions, to sculpture and even, if necessary, to all manner of exegesis' (1934).

Paradoxically, however, Dalí's application of his paranoiac-critical method positioned him in opposition to the overarching ambitions of Bretonian surrealism. The separation of Dalí from the surrealist movement per se stemmed directly from Dalí's irrepressible individualism. 'Dalí's interpretation', notes Haim Finkelstein, predominantly 'partakes of the individual rather than the universal. It is himself that Dalí situates at the centre, with his childhood recollections, his infantile sexual theories, the sexual terrors of his adolescence, his relationship with Gala' (2004, 125). The 'strength' of Dalí to occupy a central role within the paranoiac-critical, which Breton had once admired, now revealed its double image; 'an important ground for [Breton's] objection must have been that Dalí saw his method as one primarily to be applied in painting, rather than to "the resolution of the principle problems of life" . . . as written in the first *Surrealist Manifesto*' (Ades 1990, 126). The psychosexual maelstrom that is channelled from Dalí's furtive unconscious, which is evident in the Spaniard's work prior to the *Destino* collaboration, clashes resolutely with Breton's ambitions for surrealism; 'Breton in fact later declared that his intentions . . . far exceeded Dalí's, since [he] sought to demolish the false antinomy of sanity and insanity' (Browder 1967, 84).

Ultimately, *Destino* is a collaboration between Dalí and the Studio, rather than one between Disney and the surrealist movement. Early in his career Dalí held a one-man show at the Dalmau Gallery in Barcelona, printing in the catalogue the following quotation by the French artist Jean-Auguste-Dominique Ingres: 'He who will not look to any other mind than his own will soon find himself reduced to the most miserable all of imitations, that is to say, to his own works' (Ades 1990, 22). While Dalí included this quote for shock value, in the face of his contemporaries' 'Post-Impressionistic rejection of academic rules and traditions' (Ades 1990, 22), it also echoes how Dalí approached his art, not limiting himself to one style; as is demonstrated throughout his career with works such as the self-conscious *Self-portrait with Raphaelesque Neck* (c.1920–21), or the Cubist, Expressionist and Surrealist mélange of *Fish and Balcony, Still Life by Moonlight* (1927). Moreover, this openness to change allowed Dalí to embrace *Destino* as a chance to experience something new – to see his work in motion. One could view this willingness to collaborate with the Hollywood-based Disney as just another example of 'Avida Dollars' – Andre Breton's derisive anagram of 'Salvador Dalí'. However, it is equally credible that the opportunity for Dalí to see his paranoiac-critical method expressed through the medium of film promised a cinematic climax too good to refuse.

Destino: A Critical Overview

Destino begins with a blank canvas upon which a brief explanation of the project is given; as this fades, the names Salvador Dalí and Walter Disney appear, each in their respective signature styles. The opening canvas dissolves into a desert, with the horizon evolving out of the line that underscored the co-creator's names. As the first bars of Armando Dominguez's 'Destino' – 'a ballad about a young woman's search for her destined true love' (Solomon 1995, 188) – begin to play, the central protagonist (a young woman) glides towards the camera. We cut to a green triangular sculpture standing in the centre of the barren landscape; to the left rests a singular egg-like shape. A shot of the vista, replacing the shot of the young woman, immediately reinforces that this is Dalínian Disney, replete with a full array of his recognizable ideograms. The camera roams over the sculpture; it is a male figure resting on a clock face, which, contrary to our Dalínian expectations, is not melting. The clock's rigidity supports the male figure, symbolically conveying that he is in effect suspended in time. Before cutting to a high angle shot of the woman from above the tip of the sculpture, we notice that a bird is depicted in relief upon the man's chest. A shot/reverse-shot follows, presenting the woman's face in close-up; she appears melancholic and worldly, exhibiting a brooding Iberian beauty – features that mark her apart from the innocent princesses and adolescent women that populate many of

Disney's animated features (Snow White, Cinderella, Alice, Princess Aurora, Ariel, Pocahontas and Jane, to name but a few).

The woman's eyes begin to close, which prompts a transition into the film's first markedly oneiric passage. The woman stands ghostlike against the now black backdrop, caressing the tip of the statue; as the camera slowly pushes forwards, the statue's tip fades from the shot, leaving the woman grasping at nothing. In the next shot, the woman stands in place of the man on a blackened statue; as she moves forwards (as if coming to life), the clock hands catch fire and melt to the floor. These burning points of light partially follow the woman as she balletically spins from the right to the left of the screen, moving through a series of morphing transitions, until she reaches the face of a withered man. An extreme close-up of their lips meeting is briskly followed by a shot of a crescent moon rising through a sheet of cloud. On returning to the woman, we find her recoiling as the old male face melts, revealing that it had been attached to a mannequin. Turning to her left, the woman sees that she is on a ledge that coils upwards.

The style of animation changes, with the cut from the close-up of the woman's face to the medium shot of her at the base of the tower of Babel, from standard 2-D to CG 3-D animation. This change occurs subtly, taking place to enable a greater freedom of motion within the action, rather than to make an artistic statement; although, Roy Disney does argue that the use of CG in *Destino* is formally appropriate given 'the plastic quality . . . and highly dimensional' nature of Dalí's production artworks (Desowitz 2003a). Only by rendering the tower of Babel in 3-D could Monfery's team easily manipulate perspective, a capability that allows the protagonist to run without restraint around the tower as the camera tracks in a circular motion, all the while maintaining a consistent perspective. As she ascends the tower, the camera pulls out into a long shot, revealing that a gigantic incomplete human body tops the tower. Along the way the woman passes a group of partygoers rendered in shadow (one resembles Dalí's drawing of cellist Mstislav Rostropovich). As these figures are also rendered in 3-D, the camera is able to circle and dive in between them as it follows the woman's path.

Eventually the woman reaches the summit (or open neck) where she passes, in Hench's words, a 'horde of figures with eyeballs for heads . . . [representing] the eyes of public opinion trying to thwart her efforts for happiness' (Solomon 1995, 188). Here Monfery clearly adapts Dalí's work to maintain a sense of narratological urgency, by depicting the woman recoiling into a large whelk shell at the sight of the eyeball figures, and then subsequently falling from the tower – of Babel – that she has just scaled, rather than segue into the set-up involving newspapers with scorpion legs that is depicted, according to Hench, in the original sequence (Solomon 1995, 188).

As the woman falls, an extreme long shot re-establishes the sequence's exact topography, revealing that adjacent to the tower of Babel stands another surreal structure. This particular shot is significant because its composition includes one of Dalí's original conceptual oil paintings. Dalí's painting appears in the completed film with slight modifications, which include the addition of extra layers of animation to allow the incorporation of an animated figure (involved in fishing for the falling woman) and a Dalínian crutch that provides support for the tower on the right; Dalí's original print is also elongated by means of digitization so as to match the projection aspect ratio without cropping.

Falling, the woman emerges naked from the shell and spins in the air before landing on a giant telephone receiver. Dalí appreciated 'the beauty of functional mechanics' (Ades 1990, 43) and frequently fetishized the telephone in his work. In one painting, *The Enigma of Hitler* (c.1937–39), the broken telephone symbolizes the doomed 'Telephone Diplomacy' employed by Neville Chamberlain in his attempts to assuage the bellicose Adolf Hitler. In this segment of *Destino*, these iconic references act as literal stepping stones bridging the gap between one Dalínian set piece and the next.

After she passes out of view behind the sculpture, we cut to her face in close-up. As her head lowers, a look of solemnity is suddenly replaced with a wave of surprise as she notices the shadow of another woman on the ground. However, upon turning to locate the mystery figure, she finds that the source is actually a bell hanging in a distant campanile. This image appropriates the visual iconography of a number of Dalínian sources, most notably the distant bell tower of *Suburbs of a Paranoiac-critical Town: Afternoon on the Outskirts of European History* (1936) and the visually leading lines of *The First Days of Spring* (1929).

Entering the shadow, the woman studies its feminine profile before raising her arms to mimic the bell's outline. Then, the woman kneels and suddenly dives into the ground as if it were water. Almost immediately after disappearing into the ground, her outline appears in line with that of the bell's shadow. A sequence of close-up shots follow this, first of her hands, then of her feet, before a medium shot shows her rising from the ground swathed in a flowing white dress. In an abrupt motion she spins into the air, leaving her hair trailing sickle-like in the sky, providing a subtle example of the Dalínian double image: simultaneously her hair reminds us of the earlier crescent moon, while the hair in combination with her body forms a fleeting question mark above the landscape. Behind her the campanile rises into the sky, its elongated shape signifying a phallic presence within her dreamlike world.

The woman comes to a stop, allowing her hair to fall and cover her face. Suddenly she brushes the hair away, revealing that her head has transformed into a dandelion, sending dozens of seedlings into the sky. At this juncture, the action cuts back to the statue showing the hummingbird, which had been carved upon the chest of the statute, come to life and burst into the sky. Hench reveals that for Dalí the 'hummingbird represented poetry because the hummingbird takes only the essence of the flower and Dali claimed that poetry takes the essence of the idea' (Desowitz 2003b). As the screen fades to black we are presented with the statue's inner workings. With the clock face glowing white, liquid begins to seep from it, which then runs across the screen; as the camera pans in tandem with this flow we see ghostly white figures in the darkness. The animated delirium of this sequence is further enhanced by the musical score, which becomes unexpectedly syncopated. However, the tension is abruptly relieved as a male figure bursts from within the statue into the daylight; his motions are matched by a powerful return to the musical refrain which resonates throughout *Destino*.

As the man – who has just burst from the statue – stands with his hand outstretched, the hummingbird hovers, tapping at his wrist, which sports a limp clock face. The camera tracks upwards over the man's hand exposing a fissure in his palm. Out of this a line of ants crawl, which then mutate into a swarm of bicyclists. Each cyclist's head supports a loaf of bread, echoing part of Dalí's scenario for the film *Babaouo*, which was never realized, where numerous cyclists can be seen 'slowly inter-crossing . . . with a loaf balanced on their heads' (Ades 1990, 201). The volume of Dalínian imagery serves to complement and reinforce a specific message – the finite quality of human existence. The limp watch, as famously portrayed in Dalí's *The Persistence of Memory*, is, in the words of Ades, 'an unconscious symbol of the relativity of space and time . . . a Surrealist meditation on the collapse of our notions of fixed cosmic order' (1990, 179). Furthermore, in addition to the limp watch, the ants which emerge from the hand in *Destino* consolidate the claim that this sequence contains a unifying meaning, as one needs only recollect the ants in *The Persistence of Memory* that 'swarm on the case of the watch [acting as] a biological *memento mori*' (Ades 1990, 55).

A seedling lands on the man's outstretched hand before spiralling off and transforming into the woman. A high angle shot shows that the woman is standing outside a ruined citadel, while the man is standing within the ruins. The sand covering the ruins begins to seep away, causing the two figures to run towards each other; after the subsidence ceases the man remains elevated within the stronghold, while the woman has sunk far below outside the perimeter walls. This is another sequence that has been rendered in 3-D; however, unlike the previous example of this technique (involving the tower of Babel), this application of CGI is clearly evident, and rather than enhancing the shot, it actually undermines the audiences' ability to remain in the dream state perpetuated by the film thus far.

As the woman stands outside the citadel, she is framed by a formation of stones that echo Dalí's *The Madonna of Port Lligat* (1949). If this shot is drawn from a conceptual Dalínian work, it anticipates *The Madonna of Port Lligat* by three years, and places that painting's formative roots in *Destino*. However, it may equally be the case that, given the sense of 'equilibrium, emphasised by the egg suspended . . . over the Madonna's head' (Ades 1990, 175) in *The Madonna of Port Lligat*, regardless of its fragmented architecture, Monfery may have chosen to appropriate this particular work to visually reinforce the relationship between *Destino*'s central characters. The absence of an egg in the *Destino* version, which is so significant in *The Madonna of Port Lligat*, may in fact symbolize that the relationship that exists between the man and woman is actually in disequilibrium.

Next, the woman releases a flock of hummingbirds that darts through an open window and brushes past the man. The camera follows the man's eye line as he watches the birds fly back out to the woman through an archway. As the woman steps into view, the camera begins to pull back, bringing a stationary bird into shot, along with the sculptured head of a woman. Reflecting the Dalínian paranoiac-critical method, these apparently incongruous images, when viewed in association, reveal a secondary image: the face of Kronos, Greek god of time. This opens up the possibility that *Destino* may be set on a mythological island, given that in Greek mythology, after fighting with Zeus, Kronos 'was exiled . . . to the Isles of the Blest' (Cotterell 1986, 166). Additionally, 'Kronos was the Titan son of Gaia, earth, and Ouranos, sky' (Cotterell 1986, 166), and in *Destino* the face is composed of both earth and sky: visually, with the yellow and blue backdrop, and symbolically, through the stone and bird details.

Stepping out of the ruins through the archway, the man – now dressed in full baseball apparel – sees a small round white ball lying on the ground. Dalí was keen to include some reference to baseball, declaring: 'Baseball, it is fascinating. About the game, I know nothing. But as an artist, I am obsessed' (Solomon 1995, 188). The inclusion of baseball in *Destino* further problematizes any persisting attempts at periodization, asynchronously challenging the established Greek mythology that permeates through the film, and in doing so presents a categorical opposition to conventional Disney filmmaking. Two Dalínian 'turtles', loosely resembling Dalí, approach from either side of the screen. Their faces meet in the centre of the screen, leaving a body of negative space between them that forms the outline of a ballerina. The ballerina begins to move, prompting the two 'turtle' figures to fade from shot. Immediately after beginning to dance, she rolls her head down her arm and tosses it into the air; the man promptly swings at this ball/head, driving it down a corridor roofed by hundreds of white telephone receivers. As the ball approaches the camera, a cut is made, briefly showing the inside of a baseball glove. This symbolic glove–ball synthesis then transforms into the man, who is seen holding a billowing white sheet, which momentarily adopts the shape of a romanticized heart before collapsing over his shoulder and disappearing. *Destino*'s penultimate cut dissolves from a close-up of the man to a long shot of the original statue, which in turn dissolves to a close-up of the hole in the statue's chest (where the hummingbird was etched). Through this hole we see the silhouette of the feminine bell – heart-like – hanging atop the phallic campanile; dandelion seedlings float towards the camera as the film dissolves to the credits.

Conclusion

As *Destino* was finished at a substantially later date than when it first went into production, and by a new group of animators, it is reasonable to assume that much of Dalí's original intent would now be absent from the finished short. Moreover, *Destino*'s producer, Bloodworth, admitted that director Monfery, when confronted with Dalí's original preproduction materials, spent 'many months trying to ascertain what the movie should be, and what the movie was intended to be in the forties, and how he should complete it, [then] decided [to] re-storyboard the entire motion picture' (*TateShot: Salvador Dalí and Walt Disney a Surreal Collaboration*,

2007). Therefore, given the disjointed production time frame and the appropriation of Dalí's conceptual work into a new 'narrative', it seems Disney has merely co-opted the original Dalí artwork, rather than have it form the basis of a work more reflective of Dalí's original intentions.

Concerning *Destino*'s very existence as a short film, Bloodworth reveals that: 'Dominic's re-interpretation . . . of [the] storyboards, allowed us to move from frame to frame, from image to image, because Dalí had only given us a very loose roadmap to the motion picture' (*TateShot: Salvador Dalí and Walt Disney a Surreal Collaboration*, 2007). It is here that we find a root incompatibility between the uncompromising Dalínian perspective and the story-oriented Disney. In Bloodworth's words, the 'roadmap' provided by Dalí did not equate to a film in the conventional mould. Bloodworth argues that a conformist narrative *must* exist within Dalí's conceptual work, and to find it one must follow the Dalínian roadmap. This could not be further from the surrealist, and Dalínian, ideal; a surrealist, and Dalínian, ideal which sees the 'structure of sequences [as] poetic rather than narrative, often working through a specifically filmic use of metaphor' (Dean 2001, 242). Or, as Finkelstein observes, the fundamental conceit of the 'pure Surrealist film' is that it exists solely as a ' "succession of Surrealist images" and "oneiric scenarios" ' (1996, 130). While *Destino* has been fashioned into a love story of sorts, the finished film unwinds enigmatically, resisting simple interpretation, a fact that goes some way to uphold Dalí's desire for *Destino* to be incomprehensible.

Destino breaks with the Studio's traditional animated 'realism' by incorporating several of Dalí's original overriding creative ambitions, the most noteworthy being the way the film 'moves'. Perhaps partially borne of the necessity to incorporate, and to make the audience aware of the inclusion of, Dalí's original oil paintings (Disney stresses that five are present in the completed film), the method of frame-to-frame transition in *Destino* is unique within the Disney canon. Rather than adopt wholesale a fluid, imperceptible frame transition, *Destino*, in parts, unwinds, via brief dissolves from contiguously related stills – stills that do not represent the conventional full coverage of inanimate positions. This visual motion has the effect of creating a lazy, dreamlike quality, where images appear to morph before our eyes. It was Dalí's original intention to have *Destino* move in this manner, at least in parts, as Hench reveals: 'in our meetings we discussed the idea of one form morphing into another' (Desowitz 2003b). This aesthetic quality is particularly surrealist, given that it forces the viewer to consciously accept two momentarily competing images. In practice, this constantly reminds the viewers of their position, forcing them to adopt an active viewing position, rather than the spectatorial passivity encouraged in much of the Studio's animation. This effectively conditions the audience to question what they see, psychologically priming (unsettling) them for passages of paranoiac-critical interpretation.

Destino also takes place in an archetypal Dalínian landscape: barren, with a distinctive, bold horizon. The original storyboards created by Dalí and Hench include these 'evocative elements that recur in Dalí's paintings: bleak, rocky landscapes that stretch into infinity' (Solomon 1995, 188). Dawn Ades observes that Dalí's work frequently portrays 'a stretch of undifferentiated land as a vista stretching away and out of sight to the horizon' (1990, 75), proposing that he employed this style to create depth in his works. Moreover, he could then paint characters in the background and foreground in 'apparently unrelated groups and huddles . . . [suggestive of] the dreaming mind . . . where certain things may happen or be seen with clarity but at the same time other things are . . . just out of sight or on the margins of consciousness' (Ades 1990, 75). This type of setting stands in stark contrast to the backgrounds found in many of Disney's animated features. Consider, for example, the colourful, multilayered and inviting landscapes of *Snow White*, *Pinocchio* (1940), *Bambi* (1942), *The Hunchback of Notre Dame* (1996), *Tarzan* (1999) and *Brother Bear* (2003).

While *Destino* shows that the Studio *is* capable of embracing an artistic Other, it fails to represent a truly surrealist antagonism of conventional existence. It is clear that Dalí, and the Surrealists, prioritized the liberation of the irrational subconscious, and sought to achieve this through their art. Unfortunately, in this light *Destino* fails to be a truly surreal work, as its surrealist *raison d'être* is distorted by a chronologically protracted, and therefore inherently damaging, completion. Instead, *Destino* primarily serves as a tribute to Dalínian legend, and, to use a Dalínian register, it is a Disney film that could never have existed without 'Daaleeeí'.

Chapter 5

Disney in Transition

Introduction

Janet Harbord, writing in *The Evolution of Film: Rethinking Film Studies* (2007), offers the following summary of Disney:

> Disney is a form of memory-wiping, an amnesia in the face of a conflicted and violent twentieth century, and a refusal of other experiences of the present. Disney is at once its material manifestation, in theme parks, holiday worlds, shopping malls (all types of self-enclosed world), and a psychic reality spread across the globe: a banal mythification of existence as 'magical', 'innocent' and 'fun'. This is a world in which all affectual relations are held in quotation marks as a recognition that each response is stage-managed. In a Baudrillard-infected account, Disney has become the world, and the world has become Disney. (2007, 48)

This viewpoint, however, neglects the complexity of Disney's history, particularly the evolution that occurred from the late 1950s to the 1980s, when Disney transformed from what was principally a film studio prioritizing animation to the diversified global corporation that we see today. The present chapter aims to detail this period of transition, focusing on how it shaped the Studio's animation production, distribution and marketing strategies.

New Direction

Although Disney's death could be seen as an obvious catalyst for evolution within the Studio, change was already occurring in the years leading up to his passing. Towards the end of the 1950s, as Disney gradually began to withdraw from the making of his Studio's animated features, the production team, which he had assembled and worked with on a number of films, underwent a transformation. While the directorial triumvirate of Clyde Geronimi, Wilfred Jackson and Hamilton Luske oversaw the films *Cinderella* (1950), *Alice in Wonderland* (1951), *Peter Pan* (1953) and *Lady and the Tramp* (1955), changes at the end of the decade saw Geronimi take sole directorial responsibility for *Sleeping Beauty* (1959). This period of transition continued with Disney's next animated feature, *One Hundred and One Dalmatians* (1961), as Luske returned, along with the promoted Wolfgang Reitherman, to support Geronimi. However, with the release of *The Sword in the Stone* (1963), this sequence of reshuffling came to an end, as Reitherman became the sole director of the Studio's feature animation. This shift ushered in a period of unparalleled delegation by Disney.

On a hierarchical level, change was relatively gradual, with Reitherman being eased into a position of responsibility and accountability via a form of directorial apprenticeship. On an administrative level, the steady nature of this hierarchical transition reflects the continued presence of Don Duckwall, who, over time, had become the director of animation administration at Disney. However, visually, the Studio's animation underwent a sudden and noticeable change during this period due largely to the adoption of xerography.

Although Reitherman did not invent the Xerox production method, or introduce it at Disney, he did play a significant role in managing the Studio's transition to this process – it was Ub Iwerks who first realized how xerography might be applied 'to the art of making animated films' at the Studio, and the 'possible cost savings therein' (Iwerks and Kenworthy 2001, 192). Inspired by the cost-effective potential of the refined Xerox process, Ken Anderson (art director for *One Hundred and One Dalmatians*) pushed for the film to unify the 'drawing styles of the animation and the background' (Barrier 2008, 275). Anderson states:

> My idea was that it would all be one style. You'd have drawings in the background, and you'd see the animators' drawings – which they liked . . . There was no attempt to disguise the lines; I knew they were to be a half foot across on a big screen, but they were good-looking lines, and [because] they were animators' lines they always had more life than tracings. (Barrier 2008, 275)

Although not as minimalist as the animation produced by UPA, who had made a considerable impact on the American animation industry with *Gerald McBoing-Boing* (1951), *One Hundred and One Dalmatians'*

FIGURES 5.1–5.2 (left to right) Compositional 'looseness' in *One Hundred and One Dalmatians* and *Rabbit Rampage*.

background art closely resembles that of the Warner Bros. *Looney Tunes* (1930–69) series. By comparing a still from *One Hundred and One Dalmatians* (Figure 5.1) with one from the *Looney Tunes* episode *Rabbit Rampage* (1955; Figure 5.2), it is possible to identify certain artistic commonalities. In this instance both images reveal a compositional 'looseness', with colouring that does not fully reach an object's edge (demonstrated by the clouds in Figure 5.2) and that also extends beyond the object's outline (as seen with the vase in Figure 5.1). This artistic imperative, which structures the background art of *One Hundred and One Dalmatians*, marks a dramatic shift away from the conventions of hyperrealism that inform much of the Studio's preceding feature animation.

Disney, with reference to *One Hundred and One Dalmatians*, was 'said to have strongly disliked the look of the movie' (Finch 1995b, 249). Anderson notes how Disney inherently hated lines, stressing how he pushed the Studio 'into cel-paint ink lines, where the ink line is the same colour as the area it is encompassing . . . So he was very upset when he saw what was happening on *Dalmatians*' (Barrier 1999, 566). For Disney, the aesthetic of *One Hundred and One Dalmatians* carried the implication that his Studio had already reached its artistic zenith, and was now in a downward cycle; it is not unreasonable to see *One Hundred and One Dalmatians* as a contributing factor to Disney's growing detachment from the animation process. Looking back on this period, Jackson recalled: 'Walt wanted so badly for each thing he did to top each thing he had done before, and he didn't ever want anything to look like a repeat of anything he had done. This made things more and more difficult, as time went on, because there's really only so much you can do with cartoons'

(Barrier 2008, 190). Given that the Xerox process facilitated a more cost-effective production and development than had previously been possible, the detailed aesthetic that appealed most to Disney (of which his early features are indicative) was now, effectively, 'beyond the studio's reach' (Barrier 2008, 191).

A Crisis of Identity

In the years immediately following Disney's death (1966 and 1971) a management team – labelled the 'Disney troika' (Bryman 1995, 35) – consisting of Roy O. Disney, Donn Tatum (former vice-president of administration) and Card Walker (previously head of marketing), oversaw the running of the Studio. Albeit a short period in the Studio's history, the troika oversaw the completion of another Walt Disney World (1971; based in Florida), released a number of successful animated features (*The Jungle Book* [1967], *Winnie the Pooh and the Blustery Day* [1968] and *The Aristocats* [1970]), and, after an initial drop, saw the Studio's profits more than double over a five-year period. However, despite the health of the Studio during this period, the troika acted merely as custodians, with many 'of the successes of the period derived directly or indirectly from projects which Walt had put in train before his death' (Bryman 1995, 36). Nevertheless, with the death of Roy O. Disney in December 1971 this period of stability drew to a close.

The executive committee that took shape in 1972 triggered much of the malaise that would surround the Studio in the latter half of the decade. In the reshuffle following Roy O. Disney's death, Tatum assumed the role of chairman, with Walker becoming president. Additionally, Ron Miller and Roy E. Disney also had a significant say in the direction of the company, in their capacities within the executive committee. However, as Bryman notes, 'Roy Disney and Miller did not get on' (1995, 37). Much of this antagonism stemmed from Miller's inability to raise the standard of the Studio's films, a shortcoming which was a source of chagrin to Roy E. Disney. Douglas Gomery points to how 'Miller left theme park operation to others', a move that effectively 'guaranteed that the company would continue to make money', thus freeing himself to concentrate 'on reviving the moribund film division' (1994, 78). Yet, despite some initial success, 'Miller's Disney . . . lost touch with making money making movies' (Gomery 1994, 78). During the committee's governance the Studio was seen to stagnate, both creatively and as a corporate entity.

In 1977, a few years after the release of *Herbie Rides Again* (1974) and *Castaway Cowboy* (1974), Roy E. Disney quit the executive committee (though he remained on the board), citing 'deep and irreconcilable differences with present management' (Bryman 1995, 29) as a contributing factor in his resignation.

In 1977 Diseny had a watershed year, releasing three very different animated features: *The Rescuers, The Many Adventures of Winnie the Pooh* and *Pete's Dragon*. Released in June, *The Rescuers* was immensely popular, combining critical acclaim with box-office success. Its continuation of positive domestic grosses, taking $29 million, served to further allay the fears that Disney animation might cease to be; as Leonard Maltin observes, 'with Walt gone, and many of his veteran animators dropping out of the picture, there was a time in the late sixties and early seventies when it seemed that Disney animation was going to die' (1987, 77). *The Rescuers*, therefore, came as a welcome fillip, and was hailed as the best animated feature 'to come from the studio since *101 Dalmatians* more than fifteen years before' (Maltin 1987, 77).

However, *The Rescuers* carries a far greater significance in the history of the Studio than being just another warmly received animation. At the time of its release, it was taken to represent a changeover, with many of the Studio's veterans working closely with the new animators who had begun to populate the Studio. This youthful influx was the result of a strategy whereby new artists were 'recruited from colleges and art schools around the country', and enrolled on an apprentice/training program 'set up with California Institute of the Arts, the university that Walt Disney was instrumental in founding' (Maltin 1987, 77). Of Disney's 'Nine Old Men', five (Johnston, Kahl, Lounsbery, Reitherman and Thomas) worked on *The Rescuers*; additionally, Larson, another of that group, was actively identifying and training promising young Disney animators during the 1970s, several of whom worked on *The Rescuers*. Of these, Don Bluth, Ron Clements, Gary Goldman, Burny Mattison and Richard Rich stand out. Many of these animators had strong opinions regarding how Disney should move forward after the film's release; however, as will be discussed shortly, their views were not necessarily shared by the Studio executives. While the younger cohort had ambitions to make *The Black Cauldron* (1985), a medieval fantasy based on Lloyd Alexander's *Chronicles of Prydain*, after *The Rescuers*, the Studio eventually opted to have this group produce *The Fox and the Hound* (1981). Although it provided a continuation of the hyperrealist style, albeit with a lower degree of fine detail, *The Fox and the Hound* functioned primarily as an animated appropriation of the 'buddy' film.

Released in March of 1977, the package feature *The Many Adventures of Winnie the Pooh* was essentially nothing more than the combination of three pre-existing Winnie the Pooh featurettes: *Winnie the Pooh and the Honey Tree* (1966), *Winnie the Pooh and the Blustery Day* and *Winnie The Pooh and Tigger Too* (1974). In addition to being a predictable attempt to wring maximum profit from a collection of dormant animations, *The Many Adventures of Winnie the Pooh*'s recycling of the past reveals the sense of uncertainty that was permeating the Studio.

Pete's Dragon, despite not being a fully animated feature, provides an interesting insight into the budgetary impacts on creative filmmaking at Disney during the period. Unlike its hugely successful live-action/animation predecessors *Mary Poppins* (1964) and *Bedknobs and Broomsticks* (1971), *Pete's Dragon* uses animation sparsely. This is almost certainly a result of the film's low production budget, approximately $10 million, at a time when they were rising dramatically; the earlier *Bedknobs and Broomsticks* had a budget of approximately $20 million, double that of *Pete's Dragon*. Surprisingly, while there was a largely apathetic response to much of the film's live-action storyline, many saw the 'sprightly dragon, and his interaction with a live boy . . . [as] the best thing about the . . . film' (Maltin 1987, 77–8). While a number of different methods can be used to integrate animated characters or objects into live-action scenes, such as 'cell animation, computer generated imagery (CGI), or three dimensional puppetry' (Perisic 2000, 8), Pete's dragon, Elliott, appears as a stylized, cartoon-type character, emblematic of the more traditional form of cell animation. However, whereas Robert Stevenson was able to develop elaborate animated set pieces, such as the 'penguin dance' from *Mary Poppins* and the 'animal football' sequence in *Bedknobs and Broomsticks*, Chaffey appears to be continuously looking for ways to avoid having Elliott 'appear'. This artistic limitation may have proved a defining experience for Don Bluth, who was heading the team of young animators responsible for Elliott's animation. Although Elliott's invisibility provides the basis for a number of physical gags (involving crates of fresh eggs and picket fencing), it also allows the film to revert to a purely live-action form – a form that is less production-intensive and more cost-effective than animation. Additionally, in one of the film's climatic action sequences, Elliott remains concealed under a tarpaulin for much of the brawl. It is in passages such as these that it becomes clear that the artistic licence afforded to Stevenson, which resulted in a much closer balance of live action with animation, and even saw live-action characters 'enter' the animated world, was greatly reduced when Chaffey came to direct *Pete's Dragon*.

These three animated features released in 1977 acutely reflect how the Studio's management had developed from the time of Disney. Before 1967 the Studio, while actively seeking alternative ways to diversify the company, maintained a very clear feature animation policy, which resulted in the production of a series of animated films over a period of thirty years. However, under the management teams that followed immediately after Disney's death, such a focused approach to feature animation dissipated almost entirely. To paraphrase Maltin, one of the main causes of this identity crisis that plagued the Studio in the late 1970s was that the animation department had tremendous difficulty redefining its own image, and adjusting to corporate changes in the bargain; it is difficult for any enterprise to flourish when decisions are being made by committees – especially when the committee members keep changing (Maltin 1987, 78). The plight of Disney's young animators, whose creativity was being stifled at this time, mirrored the fortunes of Hollywood's young live-action directors at the close of the 1970s. Having had a period of artistic freedom (tied to box-office success), a number of failed projects during the late 1970s, culminating with 'the disaster of Michael Cimino's *Heaven's Gate* (1980) effectively closed the major studios' doors to a number of the most prominent auteurs of new Hollywood' (Maltby 2003, 180). This feeling of uncertainty and disaffection, which was shared by many of the young animators at Disney, manifested itself during the production of *The Fox and the Hound*.

Although *The Fox and the Hound* returned a healthy profit for Disney, many 'animation buffs despaired that the studio was doling out the same old stuff and inhibiting the potential of their new recruits' (Maltin 1987, 78). Internally, animators such as Bluth had ambitions to see the quality of the Studio's animation return to the standards of the Disney-Formalist period. In September 1979, after realizing that this could not be achieved, Bluth, 'along with . . . numerous animators, assistant animators, and a special effects assistant left Disney' (Duchovnay 2004, 143). This incident cost the Studio almost one-third of its staff, and, in the process, seriously damaged the 'company's reputation and pride' (Bryman 1995, 39). Additionally, the newly formed Don Bluth Productions, the studio established by many of those who left Disney in 1979, went on to produce animated features, such as *An American Tail* (1986), *The Land Before Time* (1988) and *Anastasia* (1997), that were inspired by the finely detailed hyperrealism of the Disney-Formalist period.

Visually, a number of the issues that provoked the 1979 walkout are visible in *The Fox and the Hound*'s finished animation. While the accusation that Disney was just doling out the same old stuff with *The Fox and the Hound* alludes to the film's familiar storyline of maturation, told through 'cute', anthropomorphic animals, the criticism actually proves far more accurate than initially appears. At a couple of points in *The Fox and the Hound*, the film's animators reuse animation that had previously been part of an earlier Disney animated feature.

Although this is a compositional facet that Disney has attempted to disguise, internet sites, such as *Animation Nation: The Voice of the Animation Industry* and *Mayerson on Animation: Reflections on the Art and Business of Animation*, have drawn attention to this proclivity. Roughly fifty minutes into the film, Tod finds himself in the woods during a storm; contained in this sequence are a number of examples of animation reuse. As Tod takes shelter under a tree we see, among other things, a quail leading its young out of the rain and a squirrel leaping from tree to tree in search of cover. The quail animation (Figures 5.3 and 5.4) is taken from *Bambi* (1942), while the squirrel (Figures 5.5 and 5.6) is the anthropomorpho-sized Wart from *The Sword in the Stone*. Clearly, in both cases, alterations have been made to colour and background. This change is most pronounced

FIGURES 5.3–5.6 (left to right) Animation reuse: from *Bambi* to *The Sword in the Stone*.

in Figures 5.5 and 5.6; here the lighting and special effects animation has transformed what was originally a light, sunny sequence to one which is dark and stormy in appearance. Nevertheless, despite these superficial differences, the animals' animation remains unaltered.

The changing face of Disney is also reflected in the intricacy of the Studio's feature animation. Bluth argues that in the years leading up to his walkout, animation 'was on a slide downwards', and part of his motivation to establish a rival company was to 'cause them [Disney] to worry a little and to work harder, and maybe . . . get better' (Duchovnay 2004, 146). The slide to which Bluth refers is visible in the opening sequence of *The Fox and the Hound*. As a film predominantly about the order of nature, and man's destabilizing impact upon that order, *The Fox and the Hound* has two natural predecessors, *Bambi* and *The Jungle Book*. While the earlier films open with elaborate multiplane sequences, *The Fox and the Hound*'s establishing animation uses multiplane only briefly, instead developing (limited) depth through its stylized background art. This difference is also reflected in how the camera moves through these opening frames. Whereas the forward and backward 'tracking movement' through the dense foliage of both *Bambi* and *The Jungle Book* serves to dramatically establish the natural world as a pervasive supporting character, the predominantly lateral motion in *The Fox and the Hound*'s opening few minutes does little more than establish the forest as the surface upon which the film will be played out.

Another area in which *The Fox and the Hound* reveals its budgetary limitations is in its effects animation. In short, effects animation takes place after the character and background animation has been finalized, and can be used to either increase the realism of a sequence or to exaggerate certain aspects of the visual in a cartoonish manner. In *The Fox and the Hound*, and in Disney animation more generally, the main purpose of effects animation is to increase the level of realism. The most common and visible examples of effects animation are fire, smoke, water, rain and snow, all of which can be seen recurrently throughout Disney's animated oeuvre. Furthermore, many of the processes underlying the Studio's animated effects are the result of Ub Iwerks's innovation. Of Iwerks's creativity during the 1950s, Richard Edlund recalls:

> All the studios during that time usually had special photographic effects departments – MGM, Paramount, Universal, Fox – and they were competitive, and everybody was very secretive about the processes they came up with. Whenever somebody created something, and it was the

first time it was done, soon people would be able to look at it and be able to deduce how it was made. You can always take something apart once it's made, but building it is a whole different thing. Today people are copying things that Ub [Iwerks] either stumbled upon or thought through, and it's interesting how much of what he did has become part of the grammar of film. (Iwerks and Kenworthy 2001, 197)

However, as *The Fox and the Hound* proves, the application of animated effects throughout the Studio's films is far from consistent.

When comparing rainfall in *The Fox and the Hound* and *Bambi*, a dramatic difference can be seen between how the two films portray the impact of raindrops upon a solid surface. John Halas and Harold Whitaker comment that the animation of rain 'almost certainly needs single frame animation for a realistic effect. It also needs a fairly long repeat if not to appear too mechanical – 24 frames at least' (2002, 90). Additionally, for 'really heavy rain, the effect [can be] . . . enhanced by animating a cycle of drops hitting the ground' (Whitaker and Halas 2002, 90). In both Figures 5.4 and 5.6 there are numerous potential contact points for the falling raindrops, with Figure 5.4 containing foliage, waterlogged ground and a quail, while Figure 5.6 contains a leaping squirrel and a branch. However, despite falling rain being present in both, little attention is paid to the effect of the rain's impact. This lack of detail gives the effect a mechanical appearance and contrasts greatly with the effects animation in *Bambi*, where the rain can be seen splashing and running off the quail's back, visually emphasizing the adult's protection of its young.

The Storm Before the Calm

The fractured executive visions held by those in power at Disney during the late 1960s and throughout the 1970s saw the company pursue diverging, if not opposing, objectives, fostering a management style in direct opposition to that of Walt Disney. After the unrest and condemnation prompted by *The Fox and the Hound*, Disney proceeded to enter one of the most turbulent and difficult periods in its history. Although the company had continued to return increasing profits throughout the 1970s, 1980 marked a peak in this period of profitability, with a net income of $135.1 million (Wasko 2001, 31). In the years following, Disney's net income dropped by over $40 million, dipping to $93.1 million in 1983

(Wasko 2001, 31). This drop in profitability reflects the destabilizing changes that were occurring throughout the company at this time. Slowly, as Gomery notes, 'the core corporate fabric began to tear apart' (1994, 78).

In the words of Roy E. Disney, the studio had become creatively 'stagnant' (Bryman 1995, 37). Only belatedly did the managerial partnership of Miller (succeeding Tatum) and Walker embrace the emerging cable and home video markets as potential new avenues for the 'distribution of theatrical motion pictures, as well as opportunities for new investments' (Wasko 2001, 31), with the Disney Channel being launched in 1983. Shortly after this, the adult-orientated Touchstone film label was also formed; the first film to be produced under this banner was *Splash* (1984), with films such as *The Colour of Money* (1986), *Good Morning, Vietnam* (1987) and *Cocktail* (1988), following.

However, the 'new cable and home video ventures . . . [lost] millions in start-up costs' (Gomery 1994, 78–9) and generated a deficit that could not be covered by the company's other revenue streams. While attendances had fallen slightly at the Florida and California theme parks, the main reason for this deficit was the dramatic deterioration of the company's film division. Unable to maintain a sense of currency with the cinema-going public, who were consuming films such as *Jaws* (1975) and *Star Wars* (1977) in large numbers, Disney's 'management turned down proposals for *Raiders of the Lost Ark* [1981] and *ET: The Extra-Terrestrial* [1982] – both of which went on to become huge box office hits' (Wasko 2001, 31). This short-sightedness, which was a trait of Hollywood management during this period, coupled with the Studio's inability to capitalize on the latest trends, saw Disney's share of the box office drop to less than four percent in the early 1980s (Wasko 2001, 31). *The Black Hole* (1979), an attempt to exploit the popularity of space-based films like *Star Wars* and *Star Trek: The Motion Picture* (1979), returned only a minimal profit for the out-of-touch Disney.

However, the situation was much worse for the Studio's animation. Between 11 July 1981 and 23 July 1985, there was a four-year hiatus between the theatrical release of a Disney animated feature, the second longest pause between releases in the company's history; only the gap between *The Rescuers* (22 June 1977) and *The Fox and the Hound* (10 July 1981) is longer. Furthermore, some of the animation that Disney did release between 1981 and 1985 resulted in forceful criticism, with the outsourced featurette *Winnie the Pooh and a Day for Eeyore* (1983) the main culprit. Maltin captures this mood, noting how 'observers were amazed that the studio allowed a mediocre, low-budget short subject, *Winnie the Pooh and a Day for Eeyore*, to go into theatrical release bearing the Disney name, even though it had been made by an outside production company' (1987, 78). The company in question was headed by Rick Reinert, who had previously been contracted 'to animate and direct an educational short called *A Nutrition Adventure*' (Lenburg 2006, 300).

Whereas Reinert's studio provided a domestic outsourcing opportunity for Disney, many other studios turned to animation houses based outside of the United States, starting a trend known in the animation industry as 'runaway production'. Nitin Govil writes: 'Emboldened by low setup costs and regional strengths in English language proficiency, and buttressed by "Asian work ethic" prejudices, Hollywood . . . [was] quick to capitalize on production savings afforded by Asian outsourcing, which . . . [could] reduce the animation costs of an American television episode or film feature by as much as 90 percent' (2005, 100). A positive side effect of this production strategy has been the 'affiliations' formed 'beyond the conduits of Hollywood labour exploitation' (Govil 2005, 100). For example, Govil points to how 'the Philippines is now a hub for labour-intensive drawn 2-D animation', and, having forged partnerships 'with American companies like Hanna-Barbera and Walt Disney Productions, Filipino studios are providing outsourcing services to Canadian, European, Japanese, Korean and Australian media producers' (2005, 100). However, for many animators working within the major American animation studios during the 1980s, runaway production was anathema. In 1982, with activism against runaway production gripping the animation industry, picketers outside the Disney studio, desperate to have their voices heard, even made up 'a song based on the *Mickey Mouse Club* (1955–1996) TV theme: "Who's the last one you'd expect to send work overseas? M-I-C-K-E-Y M-O-U-S-E!"' (Sito 2006, 267).

Cumulatively, Disney's inability to produce a box-office hit, its reduced box-office share, the infrequent success of its animation and the decline of its theme parks placed the company's major shareholders in a difficult position. Furthermore, 'the company's expenditure of so much time, energy, and money on . . . ventures like Epcot [$1 billion] . . . had led to the neglect of the film division, which [Roy E. Disney] . . . considered the heart of the company, its creative centre' (Taylor 1987, 3–4). The combination of these factors, tied to the fact that in 1983 the value of Disney's stock dropped by eighteen percent, resulted in the growing feeling that the company presented a ripe target for takeover. In 1984, following the resignation of Roy E. Disney from the board of directors, this threat became reality.

The most notable of the investors, who were acquiring vast blocks of Disney stock and competing for position, were the Bass brothers and Saul Steinberg. Of the latter, John Taylor writes: 'In business circles Steinberg was known as a pirate who acquired companies in hostile takeover battles, then ruthlessly disposed of management. He was widely viewed as the very incarnation of the corporate raider; executives of vulnerable companies . . . literally panicked upon learning that he was buying their stock' (1987, 52). It was with this intent that Steinberg approached Disney in 1984. However, due to a successful Greenmail strategy (whereby an acquiring party purchases enough shares to threaten a takeover, thus compelling the target company to reacquire those shares at a raised price in order to halt the attempt), the threat posed by Steinberg was removed, although this resolution did cost Disney $325 million, earning Steinberg 'a net profit of $31.7 million by not buying the company' (Lewis 1994, 102). This period of corporate leveraging was effectively brought to an end when the 'billionaire Bass brothers . . . invested nearly $500 million in Disney, preventing a hostile takeover and the possible dismantling of the company' (Wasko 2001, 32). The Bass brothers' investment gave them a twenty-five percent share in Disney stock, 'enough to control the company and to appoint their own managers' (Wasko 2001, 32). The subsequent appointments of Michael Eisner, Frank Wells, Jeffrey Katzenberg and Helene Hahn, along with the return of Roy E. Disney, saw Disney enter a new phase of management and prosperity.

Re-fitting the Magic Kingdom

The installation of this new management team marked the emergence of modern Disney, which would go on to become one of the omnipresent media brands of the 1990s. During their first five years in control of Disney, the company's net income rose from $97 million in 1984 to just over $700 million in 1989. This turnaround of what appeared to be a failing brand was the result of a number of varied business strategies. Christopher Knowlton points to the nurturing of 'currents of commerce' to 'carry Disney products all over the world', the production of a 'steady stream of . . . [new] characters to keep its [theme] parks fresh for the growing number of repeat visitors', the desire to 'stay ahead technologically', the Studio's unwavering 'choke hold' on feature film production costs, and the reinvestment in animated features, as the main factors behind Disney's revitalization (1989). Central to this change was Eisner and the particular brand of synergy he developed at Disney during the 1980s and 1990s.

In becoming the Studio's new figurehead, Eisner fulfilled a role that had been neglected for over fifteen years. Knowlton argues that Eisner 'is in many ways more Walt than Walt Disney', due in part to his family-man image and his hosting of 'the Magical World of Disney' television show, which has led to him becoming 'one of the most easily recognized CEOs in America' (1989). Conversely, Wasko identifies the upper-class Eisner's 'East Coast, urban, and Jewish' (2001, 32) background as significant differences between him and the Studio's founder. However, this conflicting perception of Eisner actually serves to strengthen the parallel, because behind the hagiographic construct that has become 'Walt Disney' also lurks contradiction. While Disney is often revered as an artistic genius, this status is largely dependent on those animators who worked around him, and whose contribution is largely obfuscated by his name. Ironically, Disney's own image, including even his signature, was manufactured by his Studio 'as systematically and as collectively as it crafted the images of Mickey and Minnie' (Boje 1995, 1012). In this contradictory light, Eisner is very much like Disney.

While some revere Eisner, claiming the modern Studio's 'uniqueness stems from having [such] a creative executive – not a finance man or lawyer – in charge' (Knowlton 1989), by his own admission, his principle job was to oversee a team that was far more creative than he would ever be (Eisner 1999, x). Furthermore, Eisner concedes that no 'tension is as great as the one between quality and commerce, balancing a passion for excellence with a commitment to containing costs and reaching a broad audience' (1999, x). This particular bipolarity is overtly satirized in the *Family Guy* (1999–to date) episode, *Brian Does Hollywood* (2001). Brian, who is working at a car wash, comes face to face with Eisner, and, seizing the opportunity, offers him a copy of the script – a 'can't-miss coming-of-age teen comedy set in Wisconsin' (*Brian Does Hollywood*) – that he has written. Seemingly impressed with his chutzpah, Eisner places a Mickey Mouse hat on Brian's head before saying: 'There we go, see you at Disneyland. Bring money' (*Brian Does Hollywood*).

When Eisner took over at Disney in 1984 he emphasized the synergizing of the Studio's visual products as a way to significantly boost the company's fortunes:

No challenge that Frank [Wells] and I faced when we arrived at Disney was more critical than re-entering the movie and television business.

We had nowhere to go but up . . . In network television, Disney had dropped out of the business altogether. In live action, not a single project in development seemed worth making. There were a couple of animated projects under way, but no new animated movie had been released since *The Fox and the Hound* three years earlier. We were confident that we could become players again. (1999, 147)

As a recognizable corporate strategy, synergy came to prominence in the 1980s and 1990s; the key concept being that the various, often globalized, elements of a company could help one another to further the life of a chosen product. Media moguls doggedly pursued synergistic opportunities, arguing that the collection of 'a great variety of media and other programmatic and creative enterprises under one corporate umbrella would be a real *boon* for creative output – with cross-pollination and creative stimulation, wondrous new and exciting products and services would be forthcoming' (Alger 1998, 221, emphasis added). While it is difficult to see contemporary synergy as creatively 'wondrous', the practice of synergizing a creative product – an unpredictable commodity – increases the chances that a profit will be made, and it is this financial protection that is the real 'boon' for producers in creative markets such as cinema. In this light, animation – as product – becomes only the first piece in a larger corporate jigsaw.

Disney synergy flourished under the direction of Eisner. In 1988, at a cost of $61 million, Disney acquired 'Childcraft, a New Jersey company that owned two of the biggest mail order lists in the country' (Wasko 2001, 50). This paved the way for Disney to offer infant merchandise that could be tied in with their animated releases; it also provided a new market in which to further exploit established character brands, such as 'the Disney Babies Brand with Baby Mickey, Baby Donald, and friends' (Wasko 2001, 50). Mickey Mouse, because he is such a well-developed Disney signifier, is present in much of Disney synergy. Paul Wells, discussing how Mickey Mouse functions as an animated animal, notes how 'Mickey's iconic presence as a "brand" has all but drained him of "mouse-ness," and whatever he has come to represent it is clearly much more connected to corporate rather than animal identity' (2009b, 168–9). It is possible to see Mickey function both as a brand logo (namely through the profile of his head), and as an animated demigod, globally disseminating Disney culture. In 1989, Italy's 'third most popular [magazine] after TV

Guide and Vatican . . . [was] Topolino, the Italian-language version of The Mickey Mouse Magazine. Weekly circulation topped 700,000' (Knowlton 1989).

As synergy is fundamentally reliant on the perpetual generation of merchandizable commodities, Eisner, with the help of Katzenberg, dramatically increased the Studio's feature production. This new strategy saw the Studio aim 'to release one new [animated] feature-length fantasy every year, an ambition Walt never achieved' (Koepp 1988). Furthermore, supporting this was the fact that, as Geraldine Fabrikant argues in her coverage of the 1988 Christmas tie-in market, no company does tie-ins 'more systematically than Disney' (1988). *Oliver and Company* (1988), the film that kick-started this trend, along with *Who Framed Roger Rabbit* (1988) provide excellent case studies for Disney synergy.

With large sums of money being spent on synergistic tie-ins, the consumables required careful pre-release research and development processes, and comprehensive publicity campaigns to help ensure their success. For example, while *Oliver and Company* opened on 18 November, the film's clothing tie-ins were already in the Christmas catalogues mailed in early fall; however, 'for any retailer, producing merchandise for a film that is not a success can be a disaster' (Fabrikant 1988). Robert Levin, Disney president for worldwide marketing in 1988, offers the following insight into how Disney sought to avoid such pitfalls: 'Basically you just try to produce things like kids pajamas that have a cute cat on them that people will buy no matter what' (Fabrikant 1988). The inevitable McDonald's tie-ins for *Oliver and Company* functioned slightly differently. Rather than offering a way for Disney to increase the film's profit-making potential through the purchasing of 'toys', the McDonald's deal gave 'Disney guaranteed exposure for its films without much advertising cost' (Fabrikant 1988).

One synergistic aspect in which *Oliver and Company* can be seen to differ from more recent Disney animated features is the lack of a sequel or spin-off. During Eisner's reign, it was common practice for at least one straight-to-video sequel to be produced following the success of a major Disney animated feature, for example *Belle's Magical World* (1998), *Belle's Tales of Friendship* (1999), *Cinderella II: Dreams Come True* (2002) and *The Jungle Book 2* (2003). This spin-off strategy has been further extended by computer games, which follow on from where Disney's most popular animated features finish (such as *101 Dalmatians: Escape from De Vil Manor* [1997] and *The Little Mermaid: Magic In Two Kingdoms* [2006]), and by games which are produced to coincide with the release of a new animated feature (for example *Chicken Little* [2005] and *Meet the Robinsons* [2007]).

Contrastingly, *Who Framed Roger Rabbit* offers an insight into the ways that synergy can fail. Knowlton, writing shortly after the film's release, paints a clear picture – based on Disney's previous synergistic practices – of how the *Who Framed Roger Rabbit* product was expected to develop:

> Disney's three divisions cross-fertilize each other in myriad ways. The animation studio creates cartoon characters like Roger Rabbit for use in films. These characters are quickly licensed to merchandisers who turn them out as stuffed animals and print them on T-shirts and other products that can be sold in the parks, in the chain of Disney retail stores, and through the company's gift catalogues. The characters can become costumes for park cast members or the subjects of new rides or attractions. In the case of Roger, a movie sequel and a string of cartoons will continue to build the freaked-out rabbit's franchise. (1989)

While Knowlton accurately captures the essence of synergy in the cross-fertilization of different divisions in the pursuit of a common goal, the generation of maximum profit, he did not anticipate the effect that copyright complications would have on future *Who Framed Roger Rabbit* spin-offs.

Disney has long history of policing its intellectual property rights. However, when Eisner took command, this accelerated to the point that the company effectively 'declared a "war on merchandise pirates"' (Wasko 2001, 84). This litigiousness can be seen at its most fervent in two cases taken from 1989. Most shocking was 'Disney's much publicized battle with three day-care centres in Hallendale, Florida, all of which featured the unlicensed use of Disney characters painted on their exterior walls' (Lewis 1994, 92). Despite the media support for the day-care centres, Disney's president at the time, Wells, argued: 'We have no choice [but to sue] if we are to continue to own the rights to Mickey Mouse. It is among the most valuable rights this company has' (Lewis 1994, 92). However, this obsession with copyright management was not unilaterally supported within the animation industry; Universal and Hanna-Barbera offered the centres the use of their characters, free of charge, when the day-care centres came to erase Disney's characters. Additionally, Disney also took action against the Motion Picture Academy when characters from *Snow White* (1937) were used 'in an awful production number at the

1989 Academy Awards Show. By 3:30pm the day after the broadcast, Disney had already filed suit in Federal Court, claiming copyright infringement' (Lewis 1994, 93). As Jon Lewis rightly observes, 'when it comes to copyright, Disney has no sense of humour at all' (1994, 93).

Although *Who Framed Roger Rabbit* did prove to be a catalyst for a number of synergistic tie-ins (a McDonald's promotion, an accompanying soundtrack, various children's toys, several computer games and a comic series published by Disney Comics [1990–93]), what is most revealing is the impact that copyright had on the potential franchising of the film. Unlike *The Rescuers*, which, due to its success, grew into a franchise with the sequel *The Rescuers Down Under* (1990), *Who Framed Roger Rabbit* is yet to have a follow-up. This is even more remarkable considering *Who Framed Roger Rabbit* grossed almost $330 million worldwide, clearly indicating a large market for a potential sequel. While it was common practice for Disney to follow up theatrically realized animated features with lower budget, 'straight-to-video' sequels, a contractual agreement between Disney and Amblin effectively confined Roger Rabbit to just one feature film. As Disney was reliant on Producer Steven Spielberg's relationship with George Lucas, to gain the expertise of Lucas' Industrial Light and Magic special effects team, Eisner agreed to 'share the copyright on any characters that were created for the film. While that mean[t] that the two studios would split the profits from the film and all its ancillary merchandize like toys, t-shirts and the like, they would also have to completely agree on any project featuring the characters before it could move forward' (Drees n.d.). Unfortunately for Disney, this agreement, after the relationship between Eisner and Spielberg soured, meant the Studio was unable to develop *Who Framed Roger Rabbit* into an animated or animation–live-action franchise. This incident involving copyright ownership shares certain parallels with Walt Disney's altercation with Charles Mintz in 1928 over the cartoon *Oswald the Lucky Rabbit*; it also marks the last time that Disney engineered a shared copyright agreement with an industry competitor.

Conclusion

It is clear now that Harbord's account of Disney as an omnipresent propagator of a memory-wiping mass culture is fundamentally rooted in a post-1984 conception of the company. Disney has not always been a vociferous synergistic machine; in fact, Disney very nearly ceased to be anything at all in 1983. Nevertheless, what Disney has become is hard to avoid. Building on the stability forged by Eisner's team during the late 1980s, Disney dominated the 1990s, recording billions of dollars in profits during a period dubbed by Eisner himself as 'the Disney decade' (Letter To Shareholders 1999). Much of this lasting success was the result of tireless technological developments. Disney, in addition to an ongoing commitment to patenting, 'found many applications for . . . new technologies [such] as lasers and fiber optics' (Knowlton 1989). A clear example of this is the school built by Disney in Celebration, the company's home-made town, which was 'designed to be a showcase for high-tech and innovative instruction and is a drawing card for families building their new homes' (Postal 1996, 1). However, as Henry A. Giroux notes, the high-concept idealism of Celebration is nothing more than an elaborate façade, affording Disney opportunities to produce 'cultural goods, texts, and entertainment and to claim that such commodities have educational value' (2001, 71).

Ultimately, it was the Studio's animated features that changed most profoundly as a result of technological progress. As the computer-aided Big Ben sequence in *The Great Mouse Detective* (1986) – the first significant example of computer animation in an animated feature – attests, time had run out for the more traditional methods of cel animation. With advances continually being made in computer hardware and software, contemporary Disney had little option but to embrace the digital age.

Part 3

Contemporary Disney Feature Animation

Chapter 6

The Disney Renaissance

Introduction

When periodizing the evolution of Disney feature animation, the films released between 1989 and 1999 are key. These films, *The Little Mermaid* (1989), *The Rescuers Down Under* (1990), *Beauty and the Beast* (1991), *Aladdin* (1992), *The Lion King* (1994), *Pocahontas* (1995), *The Hunchback of Notre Dame* (1996), *Hercules* (1997), *Mulan* (1998) and *Tarzan* (1999), collectively – and commonly – referred to as the Disney Renaissance, reflect a phase of aesthetic and industrial growth at the Studio. Visually, this period saw the Studio return to the artistic ideologies of the Disney-Formalist period, and it is this resplendence that is commonly foregrounded in popular definitions. Thomas L. Harris notes how the 'great Disney animation renaissance that began with *The Little Mermaid* was followed by an amazing string of films that were both artistically and commercially successful and became instant classics' (1998, 167). Similarly, Doug Pratt sees *The Little Mermaid* as establishing 'a pattern for a Disney cartoon renaissance that . . . lasted for more than a decade' (2004, 721).

However, while this precise demarcation of certain contemporary Disney features *is* commonly acknowledged (a Google search of 'Disney Renaissance' will return numerous blog references, fan sites, video tributes and wikis), there remains a lack of critical engagement with the period. Various studies, interested in issues of identity, have sought to tease meaning from the Renaissance period's features, yet they provide little more than a fragmented foundation when approaching the period as a whole. Paul Wells writes:

While the audience watching *Aladdin* see Jafar, cultural critics see Saddam Hussein; while some view *The Lion King*, others see an inept *Hamlet*, or perhaps, a blatant copy of Osamu Tezuka's *Kimba the White Lion* (1965); some, too, may see *Mulan* as a story about a communist girl, loyal to state-soldiery *and* domesticity, while others may determine a discourse on cross-dressing and queer identity; and many may see Belle in *Beauty and the Beast* as a victim of oppressive masculinities and a patriarchal culture, while others, a reassuring fairy-tale of love conquering all. (2002a, 123)

What is needed, therefore, is a more comprehensive consideration of the Disney Renaissance period. Taking the topics of artistic revitalization and commercial success as a starting point, this chapter will also consider the role of computer technology in producing the aforementioned features, and how the period provides a site in which to examine the intersection of star studies with animation.

Disney Re-invested: The Economics of Renaissance Disney

On a global scale, animation entered a period of evolution during the late 1980s and early 1990s, with films such as *Akira* (1988), Hayao Miyazaki's *My Neighbor Totoro* (1988), *Kiki's Delivery Service* (1989) and *Porco Rosso* (1992), and Aardman Animation's *Wallace and Gromit in The Wrong Trousers* (1993). In the United States, significant changes also occurred in televisual animation, with *The Simpsons* (1989–to date) reconceiving the American sit-com and becoming an unprecedented global phenomenon; in 2005, Jonathan Gray estimated that the show was broadcast 'to approximately 60 million viewers in 70 countries weekly' (2005, 223).

However, it was Don Bluth, perhaps more than anyone else, who proved most influential in prompting the Disney Renaissance. Although trained at Disney, he left the Studio in 1979, provoked by an acute feeling of disaffection and dissatisfaction with the direction in which Disney animation was heading (see Chapter 5). After entering into partnership with Steven Spielberg's Amblin production company, Bluth directed the animated features *An American Tail* (1986) and *The Land Before Time* (1988), in which he was stylistically influenced by a highly detailed hyperrealism of the Disney-Formalist period (see Chapter 3). Additionally, with regard to box-office performance (Figure 6.1), *An American Tail* and *The Land Before Time* cumulatively outperformed Disney's animated features *The Great Mouse Detective* (1986) and *Oliver and Company* (1988) during that period.

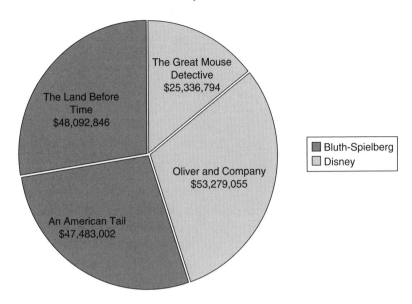

FIGURE 6.1 'Bluth-Spielberg vs Disney: First Run. (Box-office data used in the creation of Figures 6.1, 6.2, 6.3 and 8.1 derived from: imdb.com, thenumbers. com and boxofficemojo.com.)

Charles Solomon notes:

> *Land Before Time* was heavily promoted and opened the same weekend as Disney's *Oliver and Company* – the first time two animated features had been released head to head. *Land Before Time* grossed over $7 million during the opening weekend – a record for an animated feature – and nearly twice what *Oliver* earned. (*Land* was booked into nearly half again as many theatres – 1,410 vs. 952.) (1995, 290)

Bluth's critical and financial success, at a time when Disney was still perceived to be recovering from what Roy E. Disney described as a stagnant period, would have provided further motivation for Disney's executives to reassess the impact and appeal of their Studio's animation. Consequently, their renewed commitment to artistic excellence brought unprecedented financial rewards, forging the period now identified as the Disney Renaissance.

Taxonomically, box-office performance provides a tangible framework for discussing the Disney Renaissance, forming the spine of many popular

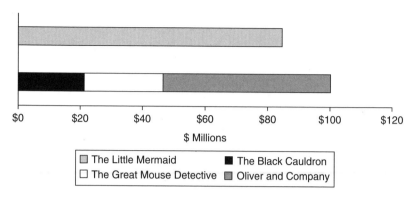

FIGURE 6.2 'Immediate Pre-Renaissance Box-Office Performance vs *The Little Mermaid*: First Run.'

accounts of the period. This is a particularly popular approach because of Disney's serial underperformance at the US box office prior to the Renaissance period; when combined, the domestic grosses of *The Black Cauldron* (1985), *The Great Mouse Detective* and *Oliver and Company* only exceed that of *The Little Mermaid* by a relatively small amount (Figure 6.2).

Despite the perceived uniformity of the Disney Renaissance (beginning with *The Little Mermaid* and concluding with *Tarzan*), when approached from an economic perspective, noticeable peaks and troughs can be seen within the cinematic continuum. Whereas *The Little Mermaid* was a critical and financial success (taking approximately $84 million at the US box office), its immediate successor, *The Rescuers Down Under*, was not. Despite sharing a similar commitment to quality, *The Rescuers Down Under* struggled at the box office (generating approximately $25 million domestically). Eleanor Byrne and Martin McQuillan emphasize the misguided continuity presented by *The Rescuers Down Under* as a cause of its failure: 'Like most sequels of this kind, which return to their source material several decades later in a grim attempt to recreate the success of the original for a failing studio, *The Rescuers Down Under* cannot be saved' (1999, 38). Furthermore, Byrne and McQuillan suggest that *The Rescuers* (1977) might also have contributed to *The Rescuers Down Under*'s failure, orientating the sequel away from the evolution that had begun with *The Little Mermaid*:

The generally sluggish and sexist nature of the *The Rescuers Down Under* (Miss Bianca looks like a relic of 1950s femininity compared to Ariel as an 1980s Action Woman) means that Disney publicity is now keen to leave the film in the outback where it rightly belongs. Such a sequel would now go straight to video. Disney have learned that it is a mistake to test the credulity of your audience by basing a sequel on a film which should have been flushed away first time round (clockwise or anti-clockwise). (1999, 41)

While Byrne and McQuillan identify a number of compelling reasons for the failure of *The Rescuers Down Under,* they fail to acknowledge one significant factor – *Home Alone* (1990), the highest grossing film of 1990, taking over $285 million at the box office, which debuted the week before *The Rescuers Down Under* and was released nationwide in the same week as Disney's feature. Also emerging during the Christmas season were *Three Men and a Little Lady* (1990), *Look Who's Talking Too* (1990) and *Kindergarten Cop* (1990), all of which registered higher box-office figures than *The Rescuers Down Under.*

With *Beauty and the Beast* and *Aladdin,* Disney re-established the positive box-office trend that had begun with *The Little Mermaid.* Although both films shared a similar production budget (a little over $25 million), box-office performance increased dramatically (Figure 6.3). While the

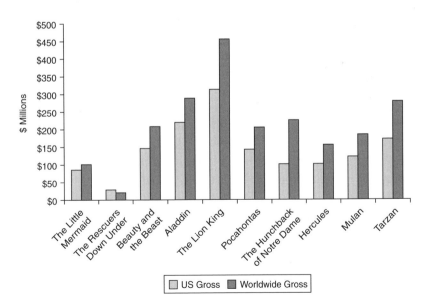

FIGURE 6.3 'Disney Renaissance – Box-Office Profile: First Run.

box-office figures generated by *Beauty and the Beast* and *Aladdin* are impressive in their own right, when placed in the context of mainstream cinema in general, it is easy to see why this period of Disney animation has been branded as a renaissance. In 1991, *Beauty and the Beast* was the top performing 'G' certificate film, and, when ranked regardless of certification, it is bested only by *Robin Hood: Prince of Thieves* (1991; gross: $165,493,908) and *Terminator 2: Judgment Day* (1991; gross: $204,843,245). *Aladdin*, released the following year, again ranked as the highest grossing 'G'-rated film. However, more impressively, *Aladdin* also had the added distinction of being *the* top grossing film of any certification that year.

Propelled to new box-office heights with the release of *The Lion King*, the Disney Renaissance reached peak profitability in 1994. From an economic perspective, *The Lion King*'s performance (as an animated feature) was groundbreaking, generating box office receipts of $312,855,561. Ironically, despite grossing almost $100 million more than *Aladdin*, *The Lion King* failed to post the highest box-office figures for the calendar year – *Forest Gump* (1994) took that honour, grossing $329,694,499. However, *The Lion King*'s effect on subsequent Renaissance features went beyond merely setting an impossible box-office benchmark.

Although *The Lion King*'s production costs were almost double that of *Aladdin*, due to an increased use of CGI, this increase is often obfuscated by the film's success. Nancy Tengler writes, in an evaluation of Disney investment potential, that '*The Lion King*, the huge 1994 hit, cost *only* $50 million to produce but generated over $1 billion in profits' (2003, 209, my emphasis). Tengler's assessment of *The Lion King*'s profitability is also misleading in that the $1 billion quoted took a number of years to accumulate. It was not until 2001 that *The Lion King* franchise reached this figure, having 'generated another $700 million in other revenue, including merchandising' (Botti 2006, 584). The trend of increased production costs, initiated by *The Lion King*, remained a constant feature throughout the Renaissance; by the end of the decade, the average production budget of those animated features released after *The Lion King* had risen to $88 million, a figure which exceeded the '$76 million Hollywood average' (McDonald 2000, 83–4) for live-action film production and marketing.

The Lion King's mid-summer release also set a precedent for subsequent Renaissance features. While it had been common for earlier Renaissance instalments to open during the Christmas season, *The Lion King* debuted on June 15; it remains unclear as to whether this was due to marketing strategy or simply the result of a protracted development (no

Disney animated feature was released theatrically in 1993). For *Pocahontas*, released the following year, another summer release made perfect business sense, given the anticipated Christmas competition from the likes of *Jumanji* (1995) and *Toy Story* (1995) – the latter of which topped the box-office rankings for 1995 with $191,796,233. Additionally, in 1995, *Pocahontas* faced competition from several other high-profile children's films, namely *Babe*, *Casper* and *Ace Ventura: When Nature Calls*. Despite these challengers, Disney's film ranked as the fourth most successful feature of the year at the box office. This strong performance (almost equal to that of *Beauty and the Beast*), from another summer release, would have been hard to ignore, and given the immediate profitability of this trend it is unsurprising that Disney adopted this summer-release strategy for the remainder of the decade. While Disney's adoption of a summer 'event billing' strategy ensured a certain level of profitability, it also guaranteed competition – a factor that is visible in the steady, yet modest, box-office receipts of the later Renaissance features (Figure 6.3).

The Disney Renaissance is frequently cited as culminating with the release of *Tarzan*, a view which has a solid financial basis. The subsequent box-office performances of *Fantasia 2000* (1999), *The Emperor's New Groove* (2000) and *Atlantis: The Lost Empire* (2001), contrast dramatically with the average performance of features released during the renaissance period. While the renaissance features grossed a domestic average in excess of $140 million, *Fantasia 2000*, *The Emperor's New Groove* and *Atlantis: The Lost Empire* recorded domestic grosses of $60 million, $89 million and $84 million, respectively. *Tarzan* is also aesthetically appropriate as the concluding film in this period of the Studio's evolution. Not only did *Tarzan* see this era of Disney animation finish on a financial high note, being the third-highest grossing film of the Renaissance, but it also represented the culmination of an artistic transition that had started over a decade earlier.

A New M(o)use Emerges

Midway through the 1980s, 'Walt Disney Feature Animation, one of the dominant forces in traditional animation, began to experiment with three-dimensional computer animation in its animated feature films' (Kerlow 2004, 21). *The Black Cauldron*, albeit on a small scale, was the first to make use of computer technology in this way. In *The Great Mouse Detective*, however, the presence of computer generated imagery (CGI) is far more visible. The directors of *The Great Mouse Detective* devised a kinetic conclusion to the film (1:02:55–1:03:55), in which the villain, Ratigan, retreating to the inner-workings of 'Big Ben', enters into a desperate struggle with Basil upon the clock's internal mechanisms. To realize this, the gears were 'modelled and animated with three-dimensional computer animation techniques, and then output as drawings on paper with a pen plotter. This allowed them to be integrated into the traditional production process of the time' (Kerlow 2004, 21).

Although the development of computer generated animation prior to *The Little Mermaid* could be seen to undermine its status as the formative Disney Renaissance feature, this is not the case. Technologically, what marked *The Little Mermaid* as considerably different from its twenty-seven predecessors was that, for moments in the film, the computer was adopted as the sole method for producing the final image, rather than as a means to support traditional cel animation. Essentially, the computer screen became a pseudo-camera lens, allowing the animator to see what multiple cels might look like at the point of capture.

Central to this change was the development of CAPS – a 'computer aided production system'. In short, 'CAPS allowed Disney animators to create their cels by hand the old-fashioned way, but once they were scanned, the computer could handle the 2-D painting, compositing, etc.' (Linzmayer 2004, 220). Although CAPS did not represent a clear way to reduce the cost of feature animation at Disney, Michael Eisner identified the introduction of CAPS as a significant step towards the reinvigoration of Disney:

> CAPS didn't save us any money, in part because its costs quickly rose to $30 million. But it did open up vast new avenues for our artists. For example, CAPS allowed them to digitize hand-drawn images into the computer, which gave them power to manipulate and three-dimensionalize characters and scenes in entirely new ways. It also dramatically enriched their colour palette. In a short time, CAPS technologically and artistically revolutionized the archaic method by which animation movies had been made since *Snow White*. (1999, 180)

The marriage of Ariel and Eric, which concludes *The Little Mermaid*, provides a useful example of the artistic freedoms afforded by CAPS. This sequence, Disney's 'first digitally painted scene' (Sito 2006, 337), appears almost to have been conceived with the intention of showcasing the Studio's newfound mastery over colour, with Triton adding a vaporous rainbow to the already colourful proceedings. Tom Sito, writing about *The Lion King*, makes the following observation of CAPS:

> The capability of the paint system used . . . was said to be the colour palette of the classic *Pinocchio* raised to the ninth power. In the past, animated characters were provided with a set of day colours and night colours with little variance. With CAPS, art directors were free to literally colour compose every one of as many as 1,500 shots separately. (2006, 337)

The technological subtext of *The Little Mermaid*'s final scene lends the sequence a symbolic quality: beneath the onscreen unification of Ariel and Eric, the Studio's animators had found a way to embrace computer technology without betraying the aesthetic principles of traditional Disney animation.

Nevertheless, if new technology is to be a key facet in defining the start of the Disney Renaissance, *The Little Mermaid*, despite the visible presence of CAPS, represents a gradual transition, rather than a clean break from traditional animation techniques. Evidence of this can be seen in the film's special effects. Mark Dindal, the film's special effects supervisor, looked to *Pinocchio* (1940) for inspiration, especially the underwater sequences, which were regarded as the pinnacle of traditional Disney special effects animation. When discussing how this underwater look was achieved in *Pinocchio*, Dindal identifies the 'distortion effects that gave a little wavering motion to the background and characters and helped put the audience underwater with Pinocchio' and the 'use of bubbles and the light patterns' as key (*The Making of 'The Little Mermaid'* [1989]). While examples of distortion and patterned light can be seen regularly throughout *The Little Mermaid*, they are developed more subtly than in *Pinocchio*. Bubbles, though, appear in almost every frame of underwater animation in *The Little Mermaid*, helping to emphasize character movement within the marine context. Ironically, it was perhaps the reluctance to cut corners when creating the many thousands of bubbles which expedited the transition to CAPS; to ensure that the special effects animation in underwater sequences remained dynamic, 'all the bubbles and water effects around the sea denizens had to be hand-inked' (Sito 2006, 336). Understandably, the scale of this project required some 'ink-and-paint work [to be] . . . sent for completion in mainland China' (Sito 2006, 257). By contrast, the CAPS sequence that closes *The Little Mermaid* posed no such labour issues.

Having seen the benefits of CAPS, both in terms of production efficiency and quality, Disney turned exclusively to the system when making *The Rescuers Down Under*. Therefore, although *The Rescuers Down Under* problematizes the idea of a continuous developmental curve in a financial reading of the Disney Renaissance, from a technological perspective, it is key – technologically superseding *The Little Mermaid*. This is important because *The Rescuers Down Under* is often downplayed in popular accounts of the period, with box-office success and critical acclaim being privileged as the means by which to define the period.

In addition to CAPS, Disney also used computer technology during the Renaissance period to help add depth to their animated worlds. While multiplaned cameras had been used to create the illusion of depth within 2-D animation since the early 1930s (see Chapter 2), computers provided a way for 2-D animated characters to be placed within fully 3-D environments. Although, as noted above, computers were employed during the production of *The Great Mouse Detective*, they were solely used to generate 3-D print-outs. In *Beauty and the Beast*, however, animators of the film's famous ballroom sequence worked exclusively within a computer environment to digitally compose, animate and colour the scene. Not only is the 'camera' able to track, pan and zoom more freely through the *Beauty and the Beast* environment because of this, but the sequence also exhibits a far greater level of intricate detail. Given the rapid perspective changes in *The Great Mouse Detective*, this level of detailing would have been difficult to achieve using traditional animation techniques. Moreover, Anthony Apodaca and Larry Gritz argue that the precision of the computer generated environment actually serves to amplify the emotive power of the scene: 'The sequence is a high point in the film – the characters fall in love. The emotion of the moment is enhanced by the visual clarity of a more realistic environment' (1999, 443).

Having developed ways to animate 3-D environments, the Disney Renaissance directors began investigating ways to populate them believably. Behavioural modelling provided the answer. Craig Reynolds's behavioural model for the short computer animation *Stanley and Stella* (1987), which contained a flock of spatially dynamic birds, highlighted the possibilities of the processes. To achieve this, Reynolds conceived three basic rules that each 'bird' – which he called 'boids' – would follow:

1. Maintain a minimum distance to other objects (including other boids) in the environment.
2. Seek to adjust speed according to the other boids in the immediate vicinity.

3. Maintain the position in the vicinity of that location considered by the boid to be the centre of the flock (the 'centre of gravity' of the other boids nearby). (Emmeche 1994, 89)

While these rules ensure that the boids maintain group consistency, in order to have them move with a collective 'purpose' a 'migratory urge is built into the model and specified in terms of a global direction (as in "heading Z for the winter")' (Emmeche 1994, 89). Subsequently, behavioural animation techniques 'have been used to create such feature-film special effects as animated flocks of bats in *Batman Returns*, herds of wildebeests in *The Lion King*, and crowd scenes of epic proportions in *Mulan*' (Terzopoulos 1999, 38).

However, Disney did not rely solely on behavioural modelling to generate the finished image. For example, to create the wildebeest stampede (Figure 6.4) featured in *The Lion King*, the desire to integrate the sequence aesthetically was considered prior to modelling. Apodaca and Gritz note that, besides the CG characters being 'animated and visually treated like their 2-D counterparts', all 'camera' moves maintained 'the 2-D multiplane pan style of the rest of the film' (1999, 442–3).

In addition to these pre-modelling parameters, Disney's animators also exercised control over the rendered output. Kiran Joshi, a member of the visual effects team that worked on *The Lion King*, observes:

FIGURE 6.4 Behavioural modelling in *The Lion King*.

In a production environment such as ours, it is absolutely crucial that an artist, at all times, have absolute control over the visual outcome of a shot. . . . While physics, dynamics and artificial intelligence may carry you 90 percent of the way, we need to achieve that final 10 percent. We therefore implemented a hybrid system, where a simulation can be post-edited to achieve a better-looking result. (Terzopoulos, In and Joshi 1998, 209)

The densely populated appearance of such sequences sets them apart from those animated by traditional means. Compare, for example, a still taken from *Cinderella* (1950; Figure 6.5) and one from *The Hunchback of Notre Dame* (Figure 6.6). While *Cinderella's* crowd scene – a fairy-tale ball – is fundamentally a vision of fantasy, animators would no doubt have drawn inspiration from the Royal Balls staged at Versailles during the reign of King Louis XIV, or similarly, the Imperial balls of nineteenth-century Tsarist Russia. Rebecca Harris-Warrick observes how, at one ball hosted by *le Roi Soleil* in *le Grande Gallerie,* '700 or 800 people were present, many of whom presumably were squeezed into the two ends of the gallery, trying to glimpse the ball as best they could' (1986, 44). Therefore, while one might expect to see *Cinderella's* grand ballroom populated with several hundred moving people, because of the labour intense nature of traditional animation, such a number was not achievable. To create the illusion of a tightly populated ballroom, large crowds of people were drawn in fixed positions as part of the background (Figure 6.5: A), upon which several moving figures could be animated (Figure 6.5: B). By contrast, the fluid, behaviourally mod-elled crowd in *The Hunchback of Notre Dame* (Figure 6.6) greatly enhances the believability of the sequence, establishing a sense of dense claus-trophobia – a quality frequently emphasized in depictions of medieval gatherings. Combining elements from the previous technological advances, the program 'Deep Canvas' represents the last significant computer-based innovation of the Disney Renaissance. Although the aforementioned developments, such as behavioural modelling and 3-D rendered environments, introduced a new dynamism into the ani-mated features, they also brought drawbacks. In the case of behav-ioural modelling, this was the need to post-edit every frame of the generated image to ensure it matched contiguous elements. As for the 3-D settings, in addition to being time-consuming to produce, once they were completed the animator was spatially confined to the ren-dered environment. Deep Canvas provided the answer to both of these limitations.

FIGURE 6.5 Drawing a static crowd in *Cinderella*.

FIGURE 6.6 Modelling a moving crowd in *The Hunchback of Notre Dame*.

Numerous examples of the program's application can be seen in the 1999 film *Tarzan*. In the sequence in which Tarzan shows off his skills at traversing the jungle, the artist's 'brush strokes' are mapped onto the 3-D image, thus facilitating a completely fluid animation, resembling traditional 2-D hand animation, which responds to the 'panning' and 'tracking' camera. As Deep Canvas combined the ability to move through 3-D environments inside the program, while having the computer accurately 'dress' the scene using the predefined 'brush strokes', the animator was afforded a far greater level of real-time control than in earlier methods of computer-based animation.

Technological development was a fundamental part of the Renaissance period, but unlike the marketing rhetoric of Disney's 'Golden Age', the centrality of new technology during the period was publicly downplayed. While Disney had begun to 'hire animators who had been schooled in computer-aided animation, its animated product still looked quite conventional – deliberately so – and it continued to be marketed as consistent with the long and popular tradition of Disney cartooning' (Telotte 2008, 162). This strategy also stood in stark contrast to contemporary Hollywood's increased foregrounding of computer technology. Industrial rumour and the promotional campaigns for *Jurassic Park* (1993) and *Star Wars: Episode I – The Phantom Menace* (1999), actively drew attention to technological innovation. By contrast, one promotional poster for *Tarzan* overtly implied a compositional continuum between traditional Disney animation and that of the Renaissance period. Not only did it market *Tarzan* as the latest 'Classic', but the eponymous hero was depicted in sketch form, as if drawn by hand. While this poster sought to disguise the technological sophistication of the film's production, one thing remained clear: who the hero of the film would be. However, from the design of the poster it was unclear as to whether Tarzan would be voiced by a Hollywood star.

The Disney Renaissance: Star Performance Value

Although Richard Dyer has written extensively on the issue of film stardom in *Stars* (1979) and *Heavenly Bodies: Film Stars and Society* (2004), paradigmatically assessing the phenomenological, intertextual and semiotic appeal of live-action stars, the discipline of star studies stimulated by his texts has largely neglected the field of animation. Despite recent efforts to rectify this imbalance (see Thomas Austin and Martin Barker's edited collection, *Contemporary Hollywood Stardom* [2003]), the importance of star performance in the Disney Renaissance remains relatively unexplored. In answer to this, Robin Williams's performance in *Aladdin* will be used as a case study through which to evaluate the importance of star value within animation.

Typically, prior to the release of *Aladdin*, casting for animated features revealed an overriding disposition towards a modified form of Eisensteinian *tipazh*. *Tipazh*, or 'typage', put simply, was a casting principle that privileged those who 'looked right for the part as Eisenstein envisaged it' (Taylor 2000, 6). Casting in this way reduced the chance that the 'actor' would inadvertently influence the meaning of the shot through any unwanted visual signification. Throughout the history of animation, casting has been dominated by the principle of aural 'typage', with actors being chosen because they *sound* how the character should. While there have always been voice artists who have specialized in animation, giving a variety of performances, their remit has been to provide unobtrusive, type-specific performances.

If, from a star studies perspective, a genuine antecedent to Williams's Genie is to be identified, it must be found in *Transformers: The Movie* (1986). Among the stars cast was Orson Welles, who, because of his name, if not performance, would have appealed as a way to increase Western interest in what was a markedly anime product. This proved an effective strategy. Welles died a few months after recording his dialogue, thus lending the film a unique, if not macabre, selling point as Welles's last film performance. However, his impact remains extra-cinematic. Nelson Shin, the film's director, recalls how Welles recorded much of his dialogue through laboured breathing, requiring his lines to be put 'through a synthesiser to make his voice gigantic and strong' (*Transformers Video Interview: Cast and Characters* [2006]). Similarly, Joseph McBride writes: 'his voice was so distorted in postproduction that the thunderously growling, rampaging planet can hardly be identified as Orson Welles' (2006, 228). Although *Transformers: The Movie* represents the first concerted appropriation of live-action star appeal in the medium of animation, its significance is dwarfed by the industrial shift triggered by *Aladdin*.

Discussions of Williams's performance in *Aladdin* rarely advance beyond an assessment of how well his star persona complements the Genie character. This type of approach fundamentally relies upon notions of selective use, perfect fit and problematic fit, which describe how a star's image is used to help construct a character in a film. These varying mobilizations of star persona, as outlined by Dyer, hinge on the audience's foreknowledge that 'the star's name and her/his appearance (including *the sound of her/his voice* and dress styles associated with him/her) all already signify that condensation of attitudes and values which is the star's image' (1999, 126, emphasis added). An example of this approach can be seen in Kerry Mallan and Roderick McGillis's study of the two main characters in *Aladdin* that utilize camp performance: Jafar (Jonathan Freeman), whose 'precise lisping speech and bitchy asides are the hallmarks of a camp sensibility', and Genie, who they argue can be read as '*metacamp*' – referencing 'other camp characters in [his] various isomorphic mutations' (2005, 12). However, while they ignore the significance of Freeman's aural presence within the film (understandably, from a star studies perspective), they overtly acknowledge Williams's vocal contribution, citing the effectiveness of his star persona as camp signifier:

> Williams embodies Genie's physicality, vocality, and mimicry to such a degree that the performance of the animated creature, and its various takes on male celebrities and showmanship, might be best described as clownish (and typical of Williams' style). Rather than destabilize viewers' assumptions about sexual identity and gender, these incarnations reiterate certain constructions of American masculinity, but with a camp take. (2005, 12)

While this assessment takes into account the impact of Williams's star persona upon the film, it does not fully explore why his *performance* is so significant when seen in the broader context of animation studies.

Wells offers a cautionary note regarding the 'visibility' of the star within animation. With reference to star-centric responses to Whoopi Goldberg's role in *The Lion King*, which focussed on issues of racial stereotyping, Wells argues that this 'kind of interpretation in some senses fundamentally ignores the visual text altogether, and merely casts 'the actor' as the condition of reading' (2002a, 116). To help emphasize this point, Wells draws on the opinions of Brad Bird, director of *The Iron Giant* (1999):

> When an animated character breaks through and becomes part of the cultural landscape, the voice actor – not the animator – is credited, because people understand what a voice actor does. What is typically lost in discussions about animation is the fact that when you watch an

animated film, the performance you are seeing is the one that the animator is giving you. (2002a, 116)

While this is clearly an important point, Williams's improvisational voice recording sessions are, to a certain extent, an exception to this rule.

On an industrial level, Williams's performance in *Aladdin* can be seen to problematize the sound recording process formed during Michael Eisner's stewardship at Disney:

Eisner's insistence upon the development of a 'script', following the traditional live-action model, challenged some of the studio's long-established practices, and had the consequence of changing the design and sequence-led process of work into one which had to more formally acknowledge the structural aspects of screenwriting. (Wells 2002a, 133)

In his animation handbook, Tony White usefully delineates the conventional routines of the voice recording process, beginning with the fact that, traditionally, the actor was 'sealed in a soundproof booth ("the box") with little more than the *script* and a microphone' (2006, 140, emphasis added). Additionally, White, writing from the perspective of an animation director, states: 'During a recording session, it is fundamentally important that *you* communicate exactly what is required from the actor during a session. If *you* don't record it, *you'll* never have it' (2006, 140, emphasis added). This approach, while heavily reliant on the existence of a script and a clear visual concept of the scene that is to be recorded before the actor steps into 'the box', also places the animation director in a position of control, not just over the dialogue in the scene, but also over how the dialogue is to be delivered.

It is in this regard that Williams's performance begins to destabilize the traditional voice recording procedure. Conventionally, when working out the speed at which the dialogue should be delivered, White suggests, 'it is always wise to first get what you want from the actor, at the speed that you believe it should be, then go back and cover yourself with slightly faster and slower versions' (2006, 141). However, this arrangement changed when Williams recorded his dialogue for *Aladdin*, as he 'was allowed to riff his lines, in the way he had in *Good Morning Vietnam* [1987]. Only then did the animators bring the character to visual life, matching both the pace and the dynamics of his recording' (Barker 2003, 20–1). Consequently, Williams's dialogue within *Aladdin* constitutes a divergent register, one which, as well as being more frenetic and unpredictable than the rest of the largely conventional vocal performances, is ultimately more influential.

In order to develop a Genie that 'would visually match Williams' character, Williams was asked to improvise speech recordings from which a genie character . . . [could be] drawn' (Wells 2006, 57). While it is claimed that he recorded 'almost 16 hours of material' (Trivia for Aladdin) for *Aladdin*, only a fraction of this made it into the finished film. However, by viewing the original screenplay (which Williams would have worked from) and the completed film side-by-side, it is possible to identify those improvisations that made the cut. In doing so, we are able to appreciate the extent to which Williams's star persona not only influenced the final animation, but also shaped the animation process.

Williams's improvised words can be seen to visually shape the filmic text from the offset. While the film's opening credit sequence closely follows the screenplay description, when the narrator (a street vendor, also voiced by Williams) comes into shot the first deviations from scripted dialogue occur. The following represents the narrator's dialogue in the screenplay:

EXT. AGRABAH – BAZAAR – EVENING

. . .

NARRATOR

Salaam and good evening to you, worthy friend! Please . . .
come closer . . . Welcome to Agrabah! A city of mystery . . .
of enchantment . . . of the finest ceramics this side of the
River Jordan . . .

He whips a jug from off the camel's back, displaying it. Noticing a crack, quickly rotates it around to hide the flaw.

NARRATOR

No? Then perhaps this elegantly appointed fruit basket
would be more to your liking? (Clements and Elliot 1991, 1)

By contrast, the subsequent transcription reveals how this sequence, or an approximation of it, appears in the completed film:

EXT. AGRABAH – BAZAAR – EVENING
NARRATOR

Salaam and good evening to you, worthy friend! Please, please
come closer. Too close, a little too close. There. Welcome to
Agrabah! A city of mystery, of enchantment . . .

He conjures a complete market stall from off the camel's back.

NARRATOR

[Cont] Of the finest merchandise this side of the river Jordan,
on sale today, come on down!

He takes down a hookah and places it on the stall.

NARRATOR

Look at this, yes here: combination hookah and coffee-maker,
also makes julienne fries. (*Aladdin*)

When compared to the dialogue in the film, the first instance of improvisation occurs seven seconds after the narrator begins his greeting
(00:01:34). As the 'camera' moves too close, we are presented with an
unexpected moment of self-reflexivity, seeing the narrator's face become
distorted (Figure 6.7) by the proximity of the 'implied lens/screen'
(Wells 1998, 185). Although it is ultimately the director's decision whether

FIGURE 6.7 A moment of self-reflexivity in *Aladdin*.

any improvisation will make it into the final dialogue, once the decision has been made to use it, the key animator for the scene in question must work to visually accommodate the verbal content of the improvisation.

Whether intentional or otherwise, Williams's featured improvisations have a descriptive tendency, serving, to a certain extent, to preconfigure the key animator's visual text. An example of this mechanic can be seen in the opening scene, when the narrator first makes an attempt to peddle his wares. While the screenplay has the narrator produce a cracked jug, in the film we are presented with a 'combination hookah and coffee-maker', which, we are *told*, 'also makes julienne fries' (Figure 6.8). The specificity of this ad lib, coupled with the clearly scripted scenario, provides a moment of animation that resists a simple attribution of authorship: Clements and Musker (the film's directorial team, who are responsible for many of contemporary Disney's most progressive and parodic moments), Eric Goldberg (Supervising Animator for Genie) and Williams can all make strong claims to the configuration of the visual image. While comparisons of the screenplay with the film reveal other voice actors to have had improvisations included, their contributions do not reconfigure the visual text as precisely, or consistently, as do those of Williams.

FIGURE 6.8   Who ordered fries? – Authorship in *Aladdin*.

Williams's influence is most visible during Genie's metamorphic expository sequences (see: 00:34:09–00:39:19 and 00:41:20–00:45:08). Again, a comparison of the screenplay with the finished film proves useful. In the screenplay, only the Genie's transformation into a sheep and his appropriation of the rhinal iconography of *Pinocchio* are explicitly defined. Therefore, the majority of the Genie's atomized intertextuality can be attributed, on a verbal level, to Williams. One such example occurs between 00:43:44 and 00:43:54. This sequence sees the Genie prepare to transform Aladdin into a prince by consulting a recipe book:

GENIE

Lessee . . . Chicken a la King . . . Alaskan King Crab . . .

Caesar Salad – yum . . . Ah! How to make a Prince!

(reading)

We're talkin' BIGTIME! We're talkin' GRAND POOBAH!

Stand Back! Gimmie some room! (Clements and Elliot 1991, 41)

While Williams follows the script quite closely on this occasion, certain utterances modify the meaning significantly. In the film we hear:

GENIE

Lessee . . . Chicken a la King.

(laughs)

No? Alaskan King Crab . . . ouch! I hate it when they do that!

Caesar Salad!

(exclaims and then screams)

Et tu, Brute! Aha! To make a Prince! (*Aladdin*)

In the screenplay, only 'reading' is offered as an explicit direction, yet, in the completed film, Williams's 'ouch' and 'Et tu, Brute' insertions serve a similar function for the animator. The initial 'ouch' is paired to the emergence of Sebastian (a character from *The Little Mermaid*) from the magical recipe book (Figure 6.9), while the startled manner in which Williams phrases 'Et tu, Brute' leads the Genie to face a knife-wielding Roman hand (Figure 6.10). Although 'Williams' performance as the Genie [is] . . . accommodated by the Disney animators in ways which [break] . . . with traditional modes of Disney story-telling'

FIGURE 6.9–6.10 (left to right)   Creative fusion in *Aladdin*.

(Wells 1998, 185), this did not establish a blueprint that was followed in every Disney Renaissance feature. However, his performance did reveal the possibilities of this kind of vocal–visual creative fusion.

Conclusion

The Disney Renaissance constitutes the Studio's second most significant phase of animation after the Disney-Formalist period. Not only did the Renaissance witness a qualitative revival in the Studio's animation, it also helped stimulate industrial change, illustrating how computer technology could be used with traditional hand animation. Taken individually, certain features had more impact than others, but when viewed as a whole, the Disney Renaissance played a leading role in helping to establish animation as a mainstream form of filmic expression. In 2001, the Academy of Motion Picture Arts and Sciences introduced a new award, which would recognize the year's 'Best Animated Feature Film'. While *Beauty and the Beast* was nominated for the 'Best Picture' category in 1991, it did not win. In fact, before 2001, animation only featured at the Academy Awards in special circumstances. Ironically, since the introduction of the 'Best Animated Feature Film' Oscar, Disney has yet to win the category with one of its own productions, although the Studio has had numerous successes through its association with Pixar. Recently, *The Princess and the Frog* (2009) provided Disney with its strongest entry in this category for a number of years, representing a return to the aesthetic tenets of Disney-Formalist animation. Most strikingly, however, was how *The Princess and the Frog* broke with the tradition of experimentation that had come to typify the Studio's postmillennial animated features.

Chapter 7

Neo-Disney

Introduction

After a five-year hiatus, *The Princess and the Frog* (2009) marked a return by Disney to hand-drawn animation. Unsurprisingly, many responses to the film have centred on its protagonist, Tiana, Disney's first black Princess. This focus, however, draws attention away from the fact that with this release the Studio also returned to a more traditional style of filmmaking. Significantly, Disney's previous 2-D hand-drawn film, *Home on the Range* (2004), concluded what had been a stylistically progressive sequence of theatrically released features, which broke with the hyperrealist conventions most commonly associated with the Studio's feature animation. This Neo-Disney period, as it will be termed here, comprised the films *Fantasia 2000* (1999), *The Emperor's New Groove* (2000), *Atlantis: The Lost Empire* (2001), *Lilo and Stitch* (2002), *Treasure Planet* (2002), *Brother Bear* (2003) and *Home on the Range*.

Triggered by a usurpation of what had customarily been the domain of 2-D hand-drawn animation, by, primarily, computer generated (CG) Pixar-esque productions, this Neo-Disney phase of feature animation diverged, both artistically and narratologically, from the style traditionally associated with the Studio. While the foundations had been laid during the Renaissance period, namely by the directorial team of Ron Clements and John Musker, for Disney feature animation to establish a more parodic and progressive tone than had previously been possible, the Neo-Disney features, as will be highlighted in this chapter, took this to a new level.

Neo-Disney: Aesthetics

In *Animation and America* (2002), Paul Wells identifies a shared postmodern quality that artistically unites the Neo-Disney period:

Arguably, Disney films, with the clear exception of *Aladdin* [1992], and increasingly in the post-*Hercules* [1997] period, acknowledge and embrace the 'gaze' in the way that cartoons have predominantly done since their inception, having only previously predicated their texts as classical narratives which preserve the 'fourth wall' which insists upon the coherent integrity of the fiction observed in its own right, while providing a framework by which the observer determines its own model of spectatorial participation and effect. (2002a, 109–10)

Wells argues that the recent 'loosening' of the Disney text is in a certain sense an acknowledgement of the 'increasing prominence of the cartoonal form and a greater trust in the public's ability to embrace its intrinsic vocabulary' (2002a, 110). Given that Disney wanted his animated characters 'to move like real figures and to be informed by a plausible motivation' (Wells 1998, 23), the cartoonal vocabulary to which Wells alludes opposes, in many ways, the aesthetic developed during the Disney-Formalist period. Although Wells identifies *Aladdin* and the post-*Hercules* features as reflective of this change, *Fantasia 2000* is the first film of the Neo-Disney period to dispense with classical narrative convention and Disney-Formalist style for a sustained period of time.

Fantasia 2000's 'Rhapsody in Blue' sequence opens with a single sweeping line, which climbs in time with the clarinet *glissando*, fleshing out the New York skyline. The urban imagery, which accompanies the music, fits closely with George Gershwin's original inspiration for the piece: 'I hear it as a sort of musical kaleidoscope of America – of our vast melting pot, of our unduplicated national pep, of our metropolitan madness' (Cowen 1998). Additionally, those familiar with Woody Allen's *Manhattan* (1979) may view this intertextually, given the musical score and visual subject matter, yet, irrespective of such foreknowledge, the sequence's self-reflexivity is itself significant. By the time of the Wall Street crash in 1929, skyscrapers were already established as industrial symbols, merging 'the tradition of the tower as civic monument . . . with the office building as corporate necessity' (Ford 1994, 30). For the caricatured characters that populate the sequence (and their real-life Depression-era counterparts), the growing New York skyline was a major a source of inspiration. Furthermore, Larry R. Ford writes:

While important cities had always had symbolic skylines . . . it was in the twentieth-century American city that the terms *city* and *skyline* became practically synonymous. No longer was the city a low-rise phenomenon with a few symbolic towers, but rather the functioning city *was* the skyline. (1994, 10)

In addition to this opening visual style, which loosely resembles that of an architectural blueprint, the choice of music, Gershwin's 'Rhapsody in Blue', is also important. In musical terminology a rhapsody, like a fantasia, is a miscellany, often conveying an 'impassioned, agitated character . . . as well as more elegiac or aspirational moods, [with] an improvisatory spirit often shaping the music' (Rink 2001, 254). The combination, therefore, of this aural style and the sequence's anti-realist animation, effectively announces 'Rhapsody in Blue' as a key moment of divergence in Disney's recent history.

The Studio's animators, by adopting the improvisatory techniques of Al Hirschfeld, who prioritized a distinctly caricatured, anti-literal style, served to consolidate the aesthetic dynamism of the 'Rhapsody in Blue' sequence. This is most discernible during the skating sequence, in which, as Eric Goldberg observes, art director Sue Goldberg gave 'the characters a flat, clear stage upon which to act out their dreams. The backgrounds become two colours – a pale blue-green for the ice, and a warm lavender for Rockefeller Center. The absence of shadows serves to focus the audience on what's happening to the characters' (Culhane 1999, 72). Given Disney's prior commitment to realism, this style of animation, when placed in the context of the Disney oeuvre, marks a change. However, rather than being viewed as merely imitative of a cartoonality more often associated with the likes of Warner Bros. or UPA, it can been seen to represent a focused attempt by the Studio's animators to creatively develop the Disney aesthetic in a new direction. Through its harmonious combination of music, animation and Herschfeld-style caricature, the 'Rhapsody in Blue' sequence provides an early glimpse of the self-reflexive postmodernisms that characterize Neo-Disney animation.

Fantasia 2000 concludes with a sequence entitled 'Firebird', which contains character animation that differs from the Disney-Formalist norm. To animate the life-bringing sprite, sequence directors Gaëtan and Paul Brizzi utilized a style more commonly associated with Japanese anime and manga – *Bishojo*, where 'characters are drawn in a very stylized and ethereal fashion, with huge eyes' (McCarthy 1993, 6). It is likely, however, that this appropriated aesthetic was born of necessity rather than as the result of a conscious decision to expand the Disney palette.

The 'Firebird' sequence features no dialogue, so the Brizzi brothers needed to find an effective and concise way to convey the sprite's feelings.

Tony DeRosa, key animator for the character, offers the following explanation for this stylistic change: 'The sprite presented a unique challenge to me . . . As she is mute, all her emotions and reactions are expressed through movement. The eyes, of course, are the windows of the soul, and I had her eye[s] . . . to work with' (Culhane 1999, 160). A less artistic *raison d'être* could be that the 'Firebird' sequence was included as a way of covering as many stylistic bases as possible, in an attempt to broaden the global appeal of *Fantasia 2000*; in Eastern markets, such as Japan, animation has a strong cultural identity, with artistic traditions that have developed beyond the influence of Disney animation. Although *Fantasia 2000* represents a watershed moment for the Disney studio, diverging aesthetically from the conservative and conventionally realist animation of Disney's earlier features, when viewed in the context of the Neo-Disney period it constitutes little more than a divergent stepping stone – especially when compared to *The Emperor's New Groove*, Disney's next animated feature.

The Emperor's New Groove owes much to the art of legendary animators such as Joseph Barbera, William Hanna, Tex Avery and Chuck Jones. However, the film's cartoonal nature may, in some part, be a reflection of its protracted development. It was originally conceived as a sweeping musical drama in the Disney Renaissance mould, provisionally titled 'Kingdom of the Sun' (reflecting the film's Incan setting), but directorial changes interrupted production. To keep the animators together while production was in limbo, the film's crew helped with *Fantasia 2000*'s 'Rhapsody in Blue' segment – a diversion which, given the distinctly un-Disneylike nature of the project, may have acted as a catalyst for *The Emperor's New Groove*'s cartoonality.

Comedy, within the Disney animated feature, is commonly located in the actions of sidekicks, whose pratfalls remain faithful to contextual and narratological verisimilitude. This is a well-established device, and 'sidekicks like Lefou (French for 'the fool'), Smee, Scuttle, and Ed the hyena' who populate Disney's films are, as Don Hahn observes, 'just along for the laughs' (1996, 20). The cartoonality of *The Emperor's New Groove* opens up new possibilities for visual humour. One spectacularly 'un-Disneylike' moment of humour revolves around a sequence of comic cartoonal reversals, involving Kuzco, a squirrel, and a pack of sleeping panthers. First, Kuzco, who is walking alone through the South American Rainforest, hears a growl that prompts him to retreat in fear, only for a harmless squirrel to appear; to conclude this initial reversal the squirrel generously offers an acorn to the trembling llama. After turning his nose up at

FIGURE 7.1   A red balloon becomes a voodoo doll in *The Emperor's New Groove.*

the squirrel's kindness, Kuzco falls down a concealed embankment, land-ing in the midst of a pack of sleeping panthers. Luckily, his fall does not wake the pack. However, at this point the squirrel re-emerges, and, in classic cartoon style, delivers a further reversal, inflating a red tubular balloon and modelling it into a llama, before popping the quasi-voodoo doll with a nearby thorn (Figure 7.1). To both the squirrel's and Kuzco's surprise, the bursting balloon fails to wake the panthers. Kuzco's reprieve is only temporary, however, as his defiant laughter – acting as a fitting cartoonal conclusion – wakes the sleeping pack.

Although anthropomorphosized animals can, and do, provide a nar-ratological space in which to situate comedy, some animals actively prob-lematize this paradigm. Wells argues against an oversimplification of Disney anthropomorphosis, claiming that it overlooks how the Studio's artists, like many others working in animation, 'engage with animals in a highly serious way in a spirit of representing animals on terms and condi-tions that both recognize the complexities and presence of animality and the ways it is best revealed through animation' (2009b, 77). Wells draws on *Brother Bear*, the penultimate Neo-Disney feature, as an example of this. The transformation of Kenai, the film's protagonist, into a small bear, rather than simply serving as the basis for some anthropomorphic comedy, actually presents a point of view – that of a bear – which challenges 'the assumptions about the bear's place both within the animal kingdom and in relation to humankind' (Wells 2009b, 45). Furthermore, concerning the film's conclusion, Wells writes:

> In this 'story of a boy who became a man by becoming a bear,' the mythic infrastructure has enabled a genuinely surprising ending in the sense that Kenai, in *not* returning to human form, renounces difference and opposition between humankind and animal and accepts the 'psychic identity' or 'mystical participation' with the animal, here made literal and authentic by the animated form, and achieves a model of assimilation that proves the essential sameness of living creatures in the primal order, now lost to the contemporary world. (2009b, 47)

Despite occasional lapses into more conventional anthropomorphic territory, *Brother Bear* provides another example of Neo-Disney filmmaking's divergence from the traditions of earlier Disney feature animation.

Returning to *The Emperor's New Groove*, Kuzco and Pacha's attempt to cross a dilapidated rope bridge can be seen to further disrupt traditional Disney hyperrealism. Given the film's prevailing cartoonal aesthetic, we anticipate that this bridge will collapse, which it does. What is still surprising, however, is the manner in which this happens. When the bridge finally fails, we are provided with a clear example of cartoonal physics, as we see both Kuzco and Pacha defy gravity by hovering unsupported in mid-air a full two seconds after the bridge gives way. While this is a commonplace occurrence in the cartoon world, it marks a definite departure from the studio's established conventions of realism.

The Emperor's New Groove also breaks new ground by being the first Disney animated feature to depict a woman in an advanced state of pregnancy (Figure 7.2). Chicha's expectant body breaks dramatically with the standard asexuality of Disney animation, symbolizing a new maturity in tackling such issues as reproduction; Mr Stork, who delivered Dumbo *par avion*, is Chicha's only notable predecessor.

Both *Atlantis: The Lost Empire* and *Lilo and Stitch* also contain deviations from standard Disney physiognomy. In *Atlantis: The Lost Empire* this is evident in the uncommon angularity, particularly in facial and muscular definition of the film's characters. This specific stylization reflects the individual influence of Mike Mignola during production. Mignola, most famous for his comic book creation Hellboy (an angular red demon), influenced many of the film's animators, including John Pomeroy, who

FIGURE 7.2   The expectant Chicha in *The Emperor's New Groove.*

was given the task of drawing Milo: 'The Milo character has a kind of angularity about him that's very refreshing . . . I knew how the mouth and eyes should look. Mignola's style was challenging and fun. I didn't have to worry if the anatomy was correct as long as I had a good graphic representation of the structure' (Anon 2002). Lisa Keene, the film's background supervisor, relates this process to the Studio's tradition:

> Over the years, we have gotten very used to putting a lot of detail and rendering into our backgrounds. With this film, the style dictated that we use restraint. Mignola's graphic style meant we had to go back to the basics of our training and rediscover how important lighting patterns and shadows are to a scene and to describing form and environment. Even though an object is flat and graphic, it can still have a lot of depth if you give it the right values and atmospheric perspective. (Anon 2002)

Ultimately, Disney's incorporation of this aesthetic led to the coining of the term 'Disnola' to reflect the unique styling of *Atlantis: The Lost Empire.*

Similarly, for *Lilo and Stitch*, co-writer and director Chris Sanders had a very personal vision of how the film should look. To ensure maximum clarity when pitching the film to the Disney hierarchy, Sanders made a book that presented everything the way he imagined it. Thomas Schumacher, then President of the Walt Disney Feature Animation division, found Sanders's vision so refreshing that he 'fell in love with it' and 'wanted to make a movie . . . that looked like a Chris Sanders drawing' (*Lilo and Stitch*, 'The Look of Lilo and Stitch Special Feature', 2002). Consequently, the animation in *Lilo and Stitch* departs from Disney-Formalist hyperrealism, favouring instead a more weighted and rounded aesthetic.

This commitment to Sanders's aesthetic is clearly visible during the characters' short motorcycle journey (Figure 7.3). During this sequence, the figures that occupy the foreground all possess rounded heads and bottom-heavy limbs (though not all are visible). Secondly, their motorcycle sports softly shaped headlights, dials, wheel guards and a rounded fuselage. In contrast with the clarity of the foreground, the two layers of background, which are composed using hazy watercolour, soften the image as a whole, reducing the angularity of the distant mountains.

Ironically, the rounded nature of *Lilo and Stitch* could be seen, to a certain extent, as a return to a much earlier style of animation, one that was prevalent during Walt Disney's early stewardship of the studio. This parallel

FIGURE 7.3   Chris Sanders's aesthetic vision in *Lilo and Stitch.*

is recognized by co-writer and director Dean DeBlois, who observes: 'I think *Lilo* is . . . reminiscent of early designs from the thirties and forties where round and appealing were the requisites' (*Lilo and Stitch*, 'The Look of Lilo and Stitch Special Feature', 2002). However, the individuality of the aesthetic vision that underpins both *Lilo and Stitch* and *Atlantis: The Lost Empire* sees them break with Disney-Formalist convention, such as the emphasis on believability, which characterizes much of the Studio's earlier animation. In the case of *Lilo and Stitch*, although acute water retention could be considered a believable 'cause' of the human character's bodily swelling, it is unlikely that such a clinical explanation of their visual condition would have appealed to the Disney executive.

As is frequently the case when periodizing a distinct body of film, within that grouping peaks and troughs will exist, and in this respect the Neo-Disney period is no different. Following the release of *Lilo and Stitch* the Studio released *Treasure Planet* and *Brother Bear*, both of which marked a return to a more hyperrealist mode of animation and placed a stronger emphasis on traditional narrative continuity. However, with the release of *Home on the Range*, the Studio returned to a more divergent style of filmmaking.

As an animated western, *Home on the Range* has only three generic antecedents within Disney's feature animation corpus: *The Three Caballeros* (1944), 'The Martins and the Coys' from *Make Mine Music* (1946) and the 'Pecos Bill' section from *Melody Time* (1948). While *Home on the Range* relies on a linear narrative, concerned with the main characters' personal developments, the western genre is self-reflexively developed in order to create the film's stylized world.

Approximately fifteen minutes into *Home on the Range*, Buck, the sheriff's narcissistic horse, reveals his idealized self-image through a daydream sequence. While the viewer has no way of knowing that this is a daydream from the outset, there are clues to indicate that this sequence may not be what it seems. In addition to Mrs Calloway's observation that Buck 'is a legend in his own *mind*', the aspect ratio changes from 1.85:1 to 2.35:1 as the camera tilts up towards the sun. The switching of aspect ratio in *Home on the Range* is not the first instance of this in a Disney feature animation, as *Brother Bear* features a similar transition, changing from 1.66:1 to 2.35:1, to reinforce Kenai's altered circumstances and perspective. However, in the case of *Home on the Range*, the switch to CinemaScope signals a temporary transition to a wider, more 'cinematic' spectacle.

The significance of this scene is not that it is a daydream, but rather that its filmic vocabulary pays homage to the 'spaghetti western' subgenre. Musically, Buck's reverie begins with a rasping rattle, which is quickly accompanied by the sound of a reverberating electric guitar. These sounds, coupled with the deeply accented, intermittent choral chanting, create an acoustic landscape evocative of Ennio Morricone's 'Per Qualche Dollaro in Piú' (the theme song for a *For a Few Dollars More* [1965]) and 'As a Judgement' (from *Once Upon a Time in the West* [1968]). The change in colour palette, from a wide range to an arid spectrum, full of yellows and oranges, also helps to establish the 'spaghetti western' aesthetic. Buck's appearance in extreme close-up, with the camera's focus directly on his eyes, creates further parallels with the 'spaghetti western' genre, particularly the iconic framing of Sergio Leone's 'Man With No Name' protagonist – played by Clint Eastwood. This allusion is heightened further still by the way Buck's assailants circle around him during a stand-off, a topography which closely resembles that of the cemetery stand-off in *The Good, The Bad, and The Ugly* (1966). Interestingly, the subsequent slow-motion high-kicking, which sees Buck disarm his adversaries, has more in common with the more contemporary *Shanghai Noon* (2000) than anything in the 'spaghetti western' canon.

Although less cinematically self-reflexive, Alameda Slim's unique cattle-rustling technique prompts a temporary shift to a more surreal aesthetic. Responding to Slim's yodelling, the hypnotized cattle follow the music, much in the same way that Hamelin's fairy-tale children followed the Pied Piper. Additionally, this tactic also results in the cattle entering into a psychedelic state, with the animals becoming multicoloured as the background becomes black. While this momentary discontinuity could simply be seen as another example of the film's cartoonality, diverging from Disney-Formalist hyperrealism, its composition is also remarkably similar to certain parts of the 'Pink Elephants' sequence from *Dumbo* (1941), suggesting a degree of intertextuality.

The aesthetic difference of the aforementioned films represents a move, on the Studio's part, to once more occupy a position of cultural relevance within the field of animation. While these films are still clearly authored by Disney, and as such feed into synergistic practices such as serialization, toy and McDonald's tie-ins, and computer game spin-offs, it is in their departure from traditional Disney convention that they constitute a new chapter in the Studio's history.

Neo-Disney: Narratological and Generic Peculiarities

While music has been a core component of Disney feature animation since *Snow White*, the Studio's Neo-Disney works deviate from this tradition.

Atlantis: The Lost Empire marks the most dramatic break with the Studio's musical history by ignoring the musical genre entirely. This is most likely due to the film representing an attempt by Disney to make an adventure film in the *Indiana Jones* mould, where the emphasis is placed on causal action sequences rather than narratologically escapist musical set pieces. This prevalent action aesthetic subsequently resulted in *Atlantis: The Lost Empire*'s PG certification – the first animated Disney feature to receive such a 'cautionary' rating.

Many of the Neo-Disney features, while maintaining the structural tradition of narrative progression through song, use music in a diegetically progressive manner. Rather than having the songs completely rooted in a diegetic context, whereby protagonists' sing their thoughts and feelings, certain Neo-Disney songs loosely resemble the musical montage sequences that feature in many contemporary live-action films. Examples of this non-diegetic style can be seen in *Tarzan*'s 'Son of a Man' (performed by Phil Collins) and *Lilo and Stitch*'s 'Stuck on You' (as sung by Elvis Presley). Occasionally, a character may 'prompt', or diegetically anticipate, the non-diegetic music, by singing the opening line of the song *a cappella* (as is demonstrated in 'On My Way' from *Brother Bear*) or performing a riff from the opening of a song ('Burning Love' in *Lilo and Stitch*). These changes, in addition to marking a structural shift, also reflect a synergistic desire to increase profitability by facilitating celebrity participation.

In a discussion of the evolution of the musical genre, J. P. Telotte notes how, in many contemporary musicals, 'people no longer suddenly burst into song or go into a dance' and 'whenever anyone does engage in overtly expressive activities, it is usually within a restricted arena, a limited space the boundaries of which weigh heavily on the moment of song and dance' (2002, 48). In *The Emperor's New Groove*, 'Perfect World', the introductory song, begins in typical Disney fashion, but the viewer is quickly made aware of the song's staged theatricality, with Kuzco referring to the performance of his own personal 'theme song guy'. The self-reflexivity of this admission is further consolidated by the 'theme song guy' bearing a resemblance, albeit a caricatured one, to Tom Jones – the song's real-life singer. It is this self-reflexivity and foregrounding of the song's construction, which, to paraphrase Telotte, limits the performance and establishes boundaries for the song and dance.

With regard to narrative structure, *The Emperor's New Groove*, due to its intermittent use of cartoonal discontinuity, is perhaps the most progressive of all the Neo-Disney features. Wells defines cartoonal 'discontinuity' as 'two ideas that do not seem to naturally relate, meet, and indeed, fundamentally conflict . . . [From which] the joke comes out of a resistance to logical continuity' (1998, 160). This device is commonplace in contemporary cartoons such as *Family Guy* (1999–to date) and *Drawn Together* (2004–2007), where the device's temporary alienation is counterbalanced by the audience's familiarity with it. Such is the proliferation of this device that it is overtly lampooned in the *South Park* (1997–to date) episodes *Cartoon Wars Part I* (2006) and *Cartoon Wars Part II* (2006), whereby

> it is revealed that *Family Guy*'s writers are manatees living in a tank in the FOX studios; the writing process consists of the manatees randomly choosing 'idea balls,' each one representing a component of a *Family Guy* joke. The 'writers' are shown choosing three balls, 'Mexico,' 'Gary Coleman,' and 'date,' which, when combined, construct a joke about Peter going on a date with Coleman in Mexico. (Crawford 2009, 64)

Despite *Family Guy* and *Drawn Together* being produced with greater artistic freedom than *The Emperor's New Groove*, which remains, first and foremost, a Disney animation, director Mark Dindal pushes the film's narrative cohesion as far as possible through a strategy of cartoonal discontinuity.

A clear example of temporal discontinuity comes directly after Kronk rethinks his attempted assassination of Kuzco. At this point the camera pulls rapidly back from the waterfall's edge, coming to rest on a distant branch. The camera now remains static, delaying the narrative progression while a chimpanzee proceeds to eat a bug, which in turn prompts Kuzco to question the intrinsic value of this animation: 'Um, what's with the chimp and the bug? Can we get back to me?' (*The Emperor's New Groove*). Furthermore, it could be argued that this cutaway also constitutes a spatial discontinuity, as its distance from the story's centre – Kuzco – is highlighted through the dramatic transition to the bug-eating chimp.

The most cartoonlike discontinuity comes when Yzma and Kronk enter their laboratory for the first time. This short sequence quickly attains a degree of narratological autonomy through the character's sudden costume change; the lab coats, worn by Yzma and Kronk (Figure 7.4), that signal this shift are also strongly reminiscent of those seen in the cartoon *Dexter's Laboratory* (1996–2003). It is here that Yzma formulates her plan to eliminate Kuzco, providing an additional layer of discontinuity as the scheme unwinds in her anarchic cartoon 'imagination'. This brief, yet hyperbolic diversion, in which Yzma concocts an elaborate strategy for 'postalcide', eventually culminates in a comic reversal, as she rationalizes, 'to save on postage I'll just poison him' (*The Emperor's New Groove*).

FIGURE 7.4 Yzma's laboratory: intertextuality in *The Emperor's New Groove.*

The overtly cartoonal quality of *The Emperor's New Groove*, which is particularly evident in these moments of discontinuity, places it in direct contrast to much of Disney's feature animation.

The Neo-Disney period also sees the 'good' and 'bad' binary that proliferates in much of Disney's earlier animation replaced with characters exhibiting both 'good' and 'bad' qualities. The heroes in the film *Lilo and Stitch*, for example, can be seen to have moments when their 'good' intentions are unclear. In the case of Lilo, this can be seen in her explosive arguments with older sister Nani, while Stitch's frequent delinquencies also destabilize any notion of him being an exclusively 'good' character. Likewise, in the film's opening exchange, the villainous Dr Jumba Jookiba is revealed to be merely an overly ambitious scientist, who argues his 'experiments are only theoretical, completely within legal boundaries' (*Lilo and Stitch*). This moral bilateralism is also noticeable in *The Emperor's New Groove* (namely Kuzco and Kronk), *Treasure Planet* (particularly Long John Silver) and *Brother Bear* (Kenai), further consolidating it as a distinguishing facet of the Neo-Disney period.

Facing the growing demand for CG animation, the Neo-Disney features, despite their musical, narratological and moral developments, failed to preserve the market share enjoyed by the Studio during the

Renaissance period. In fact, it may have been this need to appear 'cutting edge' that prompted the Studio's 2002 flirtation with the science fiction genre. Given its overlap with the horror and fantasy genres, science fiction is one of the most problematic genres for which to establish stable, interpretive criteria. Moreover, from an iconographic perspective, the science fiction genre does not support a nexus of signification comparable to the western or gangster genres; this fundamental indeterminacy is perhaps the main reason why science fiction does not feature in the formative studies of genre. Vivian Sobchack writes:

> [O]ne could create a list of . . . [science fiction] 'objects' as the spaceship which do indeed *evoke* the genre, but which are – specifically and physically – not *essential* to it: the New Planet, the Robot,the Laboratory, Radioactive Isotopes, and Atomic Devices. On the other hand, it is extremely difficult to think of a Western which does not take place in a visually represented 'West' with guns and horses, or recall a Gangster film which does not show a nightclub or which has no guns and no automobiles. (1998, 65–6)

Consequently, science fiction can be seen as one of the 'most flexible popular genres' (Telotte 2001, 11).

While the concept of Disney science fiction may seem alien, the Studio's animation has, albeit infrequently, made use of the genre. Although *Lilo and Stitch* and *Treasure Planet* are Disney's first feature-length science fiction animations, the Studio first engaged with the genre during the late 1950s. Stimulated by the developing space race, Disney produced a series of animations discussing space travel (*Man in Space* [1955], *Man and the Moon* [1955], *Mars and Beyond* [1957] and *Eyes in Outer Space* [1959]) as part of Walt Disney's weekly television series. Furthermore, the Disney-funded *Tron* (1982), although distributed under the banner of Lisberger/Kushner Productions, represents another example of the Studio's flirtation with science fiction – in this case prompted by the successes of *Star Wars* (1977) and *Star Wars: Episode V – The Empire Strikes Back* (1980). Recently, *Tron: Legacy* (2010) provided a lucrative renewal of this cult favourite, and, with a third instalment planned, it appears that the hybrid of live-action and animation has become the aesthetic of choice for Disney's science fiction filmmaking.

Given the number of animated features that adopted the Disney-Formalist style during the 1990s, such as *Anastasia* (1997), *Quest for Camelot* (1998), *The Magic Riddle* (1991) and *The Swan Princess* (1994), the

Studio, understandably, sought new genres to ensure product differentiation and marketability. Despite the fact that, by 2000, science fiction had become 'one of the most popular and lucrative genres in cinema history' (King and Krzywinska 2000, 8), it is surprising that Disney chose to embrace the genre so completely at that time, as, during the early planning and production phases of *Lilo and Stitch* and *Treasure Planet*, Disney's executives would almost certainly have been aware of the box-office failures of *The Iron Giant* (1999) and *Titan A.E.* (2000).

Although *Lilo and Stitch* performed well, grossing over $270 million worldwide (from a production budget of approximately $80 million), *Treasure Planet*, like *The Iron Giant* and *Titan A.E.* before it, continued the recent unprofitability of traditionally animated science fiction features, grossing only $109 million worldwide (after accruing approximately $140 million in negative costs). In light of this, Disney's executives would have been reluctant to finance any further projects in this genre. Consequently, as a constituent element of the Neo-Disney period, science fiction represents little more than a fleeting influence. However, in the now dominant field of CG animation, the genre has proven to be both popular and highly profitable, with Disney and Pixar alone responsible for *Monsters, Inc.* (2001), *The Incredibles* (2004), *Meet the Robinsons* (2007) and *WALL-E* (2008).

Conclusion

Ultimately, given the significance of profitability as a barometer for measuring filmic success, the Neo-Disney features, in future years, will likely be considered as constituting, at best, a period of strategic uncertainty, and at worst, a period of extended failure. However, this five-year period is perhaps the most consistently experimental in the Studio's history, containing a package feature, feature-length science fiction animation, and a western parody. Ironically, given the recent success of the largely traditional hand-drawn *The Princess and the Frog*, a return to the serendipitous freedom of the Neo-Disney period may now prove difficult. Yet, beyond hand-drawn animation, in the domain of CG animation, there is still scope for the Studio to again push the boundaries of what is expected of Disney filmmaking.

Chapter 8

Digital Disney

Introduction

In 1995 *Toy Story* was released. The film opens on a boy, Andy, playing with his toys in a 'village' composed of cardboard boxes. Andy's ludic narrative pits Mr Potato Head, a wanted criminal who is holding Bo Peep captive, against Woody, a draw-string Cowboy. Despite the scene's mythological Wild West connotations, Andy reveals a desire for a more futuristic theme when he introduces Mr Potato Head's attack dog (a Slinky Dog), which, he states, features a built-in force field. With the help of Rex, a toy dinosaur, Andy has Woody save the day, successfully placing Mr Potato Head in jail (a baby's cot).

We soon discover that, ahead of schedule, Andy is to have his birthday party, causing the toys to reveal their insecurities about the fear of being replaced by newer, more exciting models. Woody responds, seeking to placate his friends:

WOODY

Come on guys, every Christmas and birthday we go through this.

REX

What if it's another dinosaur, a mean one? I just don't think I can take that kind of rejection.

WOODY

Hey, listen! No one's getting replaced; this is Andy we're talking about. It doesn't matter how much we're played with, what matters is that we're here for Andy when *he* needs us. That's what we're made for, right? (*Toy Story*)

However, with the arrival of Buzz Lightyear, the status quo is irrevocably changed. While Woody had been the accepted alpha figure prior to

Buzz's introduction, representing law and order in the toy domain (and during play with Andy), Buzz's technological appeal immediately establishes him as a challenger to Woody's premiership.

This relationship, in addition to being central to the *Toy Story* narrative, also serves as an allegory for the emergence of Pixar as a significant producer of animation. Disney, represented in this sense by Woody, had, up until 1995, been the dominant figure in traditional Western animation for a considerable time. With Pixar's breakthrough, not only was Disney's place within animation challenged, but the industry itself was forced to reconsider its blinkered faith in traditional 2-D animation. David A. Price writes of Disney's embracing of Pixar during the production of *Toy Story*:

> It was, for the moment, too early to take seriously the possibility that the business landscape for Disney had just undergone a momentous change – that Disney might have unwittingly opened itself up to meaningful competition in animated feature films. It was a ridiculous idea. Upstarts like Don Bluth . . . had come and gone, for all intents and purposes. In the end, Disney still owned feature animation. It had always been so. It would always be so. Disney would dominate computer animation as it had dominated cel animation. Pixar would be the eager-to-please contractor. The stars and the planets seemed to be set in their courses. (2008, 156)

However, as Woody's reassurances to Rex proved to be miscalculated, Disney's faith in old certainties proved equally short-sighted. Pixar, like Buzz, quickly became an established leader alongside Disney.

Recently, several books relating to the business evolution of Disney and Pixar have been published: *Work in Progress: Risking Failure, Surviving Success* (Eisner, 1999), *To Infinity and Beyond: The Story of Pixar Animation Studios* (Paik, 2007) and *The Pixar Touch: The Making of a Company* (Price, 2008). Although these texts approach their subject matter from different angles, they all employ a hagiographic register. For example, while *To Infinity and Beyond* and *The Pixar Touch* draw attention to the relationship between Disney and Pixar, their main focus is the chronicling of Pixar's rise from an unprofitable software and hardware developer to the leading name in computer generated animation. Given the ongoing evolution of both studios, the full extent of Pixar's effect upon contemporary Disney is impossible to calculate. Nonetheless, from a hierarchical and artistic perspective, Pixar's influence upon Disney *can* be seen.

Disney–Pixarchy

Despite the profound impact that Pixar has had upon the animation industry, for many, the exact details of Disney and Pixar's relationship remains a source of confusion. Although animated features released under the Disney–Pixar banner benefit from a high level of positive brand-awareness, the average cinema-goer is unlikely to be aware of the considerable influence that Pixar has had upon Disney throughout the last two decades. Moreover, the highly publicized 'bust-up' between the studios in 2004 (see 'Pixar to Find Its Own Way as Disney Partnership Ends' [Holson 2004] and 'Pixar Dumps Disney' [2004]), followed by Disney's headline-making buyout of Pixar in 2006 (see 'Disney Agrees to Acquire Pixar in a $7.4 Billion Deal' [Holson 2006]), may, in fact, lead many to the opposite conclusion – that Pixar is little more than a desirable brand name maintained by Disney.

Pixar's first notable contribution to Disney evolution occurred in the late 1980s, with the development of the 'computer aided production system' (CAPS). Regardless of the major impact that CAPS had upon the way feature animation was produced (see Chapter 6), Disney did not openly admit to the use of this process for a number of years. At that time Pixar was primarily a research hotbed, not a profitable animation studio, so many at Pixar 'felt frustrated by Disney's secrecy – prestige and fame, more than money, being the currency of the research world' (Price 2008, 95). In the long term, Price notes: 'CAPS was the seed of Pixar's working relationship with Disney; it had surpassed Disney's expectations and had come in ahead of schedule. It was the first in a series of successful pieces of work that would serve as calling cards for Pixar when it was ready, years later, to move up to feature films' (2008, 95). In 1991, Pixar, armed with *Toy Story*, entered into a three-film deal with Disney; however, 'the financial terms of the thirteen-page contract were lopsided enough that unless the film were a hit on the level of *The Little Mermaid*, Pixar's earnings from it would be insignificant' (Price 2008, 123). After renegotiating terms in 1997, Disney and Pixar's relatively harmonious partnership yielded a further three computer generated features over a four year period: *A Bug's Life* (1998), *Toy Story 2* (1999) and *Monsters, Inc.* (2001).

In early 2004, however, after almost a year of acrimonious contract renegotiations, Steve Jobs (Pixar's CEO) announced that Pixar would break its association with Disney at the end of its current agreement. Such was Pixar's standing at this time that news of the upcoming split prompted significant soul-searching at Disney. Michael Eisner, who had been a major factor in the Studio's 1990s resurgence, was soon cast, in the words of Disney Renaissance animator Dave Pruiksma, as 'The Ogre King', a 'threat to Walt's Kingdom' (2006). Disney was no longer the irrefutable market leader within the field of animation, and many attributed the Studio's slide to the failings of Eisner. While the view was almost unanimously held that Pixar, not Disney, was now at the forefront of animation, Eisner remained blinkered. In 2003, during the lead-up to *Finding Nemo's release*, he intimated, 'although Pixar Animation Studios was excited about its film, he was not impressed by early cuts he'd seen', concluding that Pixar was 'headed for "a reality check"' (Eller and Verrier 2004). Eisner was wrong: the appeal and influence of Pixar ultimately led to his Disney exit only a few years later.

The departure of Roy E. Disney, in November 2003, effectively triggered a boardroom battle that lasted until October 2005. In his provocative letter of resignation, Disney identified seven ways in which Eisner's leadership had failed. Of these, points four, five and six reflect most clearly what Disney perceived to be the Studio's biggest failings:

4. The perception by all of our stakeholders – consumers, investors, employees, distributors and suppliers – that the Company is rapacious, soul-less, and always looking for the 'quick buck' rather than the long-term value which is leading to a loss of public trust.
5. The creative brain drain of the last several years, which is real and continuing, and damages our Company with the loss of every talented employee.
6. Your failure to establish and build constructive relationships with creative partners, especially Pixar, Miramax, and the cable companies distributing our products. (Disney 2003)

After leaving, Disney helped create the website SaveDisney.com, which, coupled with growing support for the departed board member, saw Eisner's job security fall dramatically. In March 2004, at the annual shareholders meeting, Eisner suffered 'the highest no-confidence vote ever against a chief executive officer of a major company' (Price 2008, 240). Although Eisner remained as Disney's CEO, he was stripped of his position as chairman; the following year, after more boardroom pressure, Eisner agreed to leave a year earlier than his contract stipulated.

Rather than promote Dick Cook, who had been the chairman of Disney's various studios since 2002 (and also had the distinction of having worked at Disney since before the start of Eisner's rule), the man chosen to succeed

Eisner was Robert A. Iger. Having 'previously served as President and
Chief Operating Officer since January 2000' (Board of Directors, *The
Walt Disney Company: Corporate Information*), Iger was appointed as Disney
CEO on 1 October 2005. A month before his official instalment, Iger was
present at the opening of Hong Kong Disneyland and was startled to
realize 'that there wasn't a character in the parade that had come from a
Disney animated film in the last ten years except for Pixar' (Price 2008,
252). Price writes:

> The experience brought home to Iger that the Walt Disney Co. was
> failing badly in feature animation – which Iger believed was Disney's
> most important business, the one that in the past had created its most
> enduring films, the one that had supplied the characters for its theme-
> park attractions and merchandise, the one that had provided many of
> the songs for its music division, and, above all, the one that had made
> Disney Disney. (2008, 252)

If, at this juncture, Iger had allowed the Studio's partnership with Pixar
to come to an end, not only would it have immediately weakened Disney's
animation production potential, but it would also have been seen as the
Studio passively acquiescing to Pixar's ascent to the summit of Western
animation.

Prompted by this, and armed with market research that showed mothers
with young children 'now rated Pixar's brand higher, on average, than
Disney's' (Price 2008, 252), Iger proposed that Disney acquire Pixar. On
24 January 2006, Disney announced that it had agreed to terms with
Pixar for an all-stock transaction. Symbolically, Disney had taken over
Pixar. However, the internal reshuffling that occurred after Pixar's acqui-
sition meant that, actually, it was Pixar's hierarchy that would now drive
'Disney' animation forward.

As part of this deal, Lasseter became 'chief creative officer of the two
studios and the principal creative adviser at Walt Disney Imagineering'
(Holson 2006). Alongside fellow Pixar luminary Edwin Catmull, Lasseter
immediately 'brought back a handful of Disney animation standouts who
had only recently been laid off, including Ron Clements and John Musker,
co-directors of *Hercules, Aladdin*, and *The Little Mermaid*, and Eric Goldberg, co-director of *Pocahontas*' (Price 2008, 254). Speaking at a screening of *Bolt* (2008), Lasseter recalled how, when he took over, 'Disney had
got away from quality' and had fallen into a routine of 'doing things to
make a buck' (Gritten 2009). Lasseter was deeply opposed to this and

wanted to remould Disney into a filmmakers' studio, with an emphasis on perfection. One quick solution was the discontinuation of Disney's straight-to-DVD tie-ins, with Lasseter publicly stating that he was 'against making really bad sequels to movies that Walt Disney made at the height of his talent' (Gritten 2009). Finally, Lasseter identified a shorts program as a way of rejuvenating the studio's pigeonholed animators. By allowing animators to cross-pollinate on low-pressure, two million dollar shorts, rather than on features costing in excess of $100 million, he brought a level of creativity back to a studio which, until recently, had been driven primarily by profit margins.

Given the unpredictability of Disney's postmillennial animation (see Chapter 7), Pixar's features helped maintain Disney's animation-based profitability, even at a time when the Studio's own productions were failing to scale the heights of its Renaissance years. In addition to the influence that Pixar exerted over Disney on a boardroom level, Pixar's 'Hyper-Real' aesthetic also prompted a definite artistic shift at Disney, while also helping to shape what would become the dominant form of feature animation at the beginning of the new millennium.[1]

Pixar's 'Hyper-Realism' and the Evolution of an Industry

Early computer generated animation was used sparingly within the film industry, because, as John Lasseter remarks, it relied on 'geometric primitives (basic geometric shapes)' (Telotte 2008, 159–60) that appeared either unnaturally angular or plastic-looking. In fact, CGI was used almost exclusively to produce sequences that required a style in keeping with the process's limitations; two of the clearest examples of this are Disney's own *Tron* (1982), for which a precise computer aesthetic was essential, and the stained-glass knight from *Young Sherlock Holmes* (1985), which benefitted from the angular styling. However, with computer hardware keeping pace with Moore's Law, and continually developing software, computer animation quickly reached a far greater level of sophistication.

---

[1] To increase the clarity of this discussion, 'hyper-realism' with a hyphen will refer to Pixar's development of the concept, whereas hyperrealism without a hyphen will continue to denote a Disney-Formalist use of the term.

Photorealistic digital imagery and animation became a feature of mainstream filmmaking at the beginning of the 1990s, with, in many instances, 'the breakthrough CGI technique' becoming 'the "must see" narrative image of the film, reproduced in posters and trailers' (Redmond 2009, 139). In the case of *Terminator 2: Judgment Day* (1991), the film's 'morphing technique, enabling "live" actor Robert Patrick and T-1000 liquid metal Terminator seamlessly to merge and blend, was marketed as the central experiential pull of the film' (Redmond 2009, 139). Conversely, the year after *Terminator 2*'s release, CGI was used on the film *Death Becomes Her* (1992) with a very different aim: to create photo-realistic skin that did not overtly 'announce' itself as a special effect, allowing Madeline's reversed head to appear believable. Although CG animation crept slowly into the vocabulary of mainstream cinema, the 'inclusion of over fifty CGI shots (approximately six and a half minutes of screen time) in *Jurassic Park* [1993] marked the technology's first wide-scale usage and essentially consigned stop-motion miniature techniques to the bin of historical artefacts' (Friedman 2006, 133). In addition to the photo*realism* – or, more accurately, 'believability' – of the dinosaurs in *Jurassic Park*, Kathi Jackson suggests that 'using CGI saved the studio $10 million' (Jackson 2007, 53). However, the increased sophistication of digital animation forced filmmakers to reconsider how it impacted on spectatorial investment, with particular reference to the viewer's enjoyment of the digital image.

In 1970, Masahiro Mori described a phenomenon that has become known as the 'uncanny valley'. Mori, although primarily concerned with the design of humanlike robots, observed that the more a robot begins to resemble a human, the more we are likely to feel an affinity towards it, resulting in a relationship that can be represented by the equation $y = f(x)$; simply put, this equation denotes that 'the value of y [affinity] increases (or decreases) continuously with the value of x [human likeness]' (1970, 33). However, drawing on contemporary advances in prosthetics as an example, Mori outlined a problem with the applicability of this equation to the development of human-like robots:

[P]rosthetic hands have improved greatly . . . Some prosthetic hands attempt to simulate veins, muscles, tendons, finger nails, and finger prints, and their colour resembles human pigmentation. . . . But this kind of prosthetic hand is too real and when we notice it is prosthetic, we have a sense of strangeness. So if we shake the hand, we are surprised by the lack of soft tissue and cold temperature. In this case, there is no longer a sense of familiarity. It is uncanny. (1970, 34)

Mori also noted that as the human likeness nears perfection, affinity once again increases, reaching a level that exceeds that which had been achieved before the uncanny moment. When plotted on a graph, this sudden loss of affinity represents a deep trough – the 'uncanny valley'.

Although Mori's discussion pertains to the field of robotics, his findings also carry strong implications for digital cinema. Not only is the concept explored on a textual level in the films *Blade Runner* (1982) and *S1m0ne* (2002), but Mori's theory has also had an effect on how certain digitally created films look. While examples of photorealistic digital animation were 'visible' in a number of live-action films released prior to, or during, the development of *Toy Story*, Catmull was reluctant to have Pixar subscribe to a similar aesthetic: 'The problem is, the closer you get to reality, that's when the brain starts to kick in with its auto-recognizers, and thinks something is a little weird' (Telotte 2008, 160). In order to satisfactorily negotiate this psychological issue, Pixar developed their own form of hyper-realism.

So far in this book, hyperrealism has denoted a style of cel animation, founded during the Disney-Formalist period, which prioritizes believability and aspires to present 'verisimilitude in . . . characters, contexts and narratives' (Wells 1998, 23). In this sense, the animator works *towards* a construction of 'realism', while constantly knowing that whatever he achieves will ultimately be only a gradation of reality, moderated by the overt artificiality of the medium itself. However, for Pixar's animators, computer technology affords a far greater level of control over the finished image than is available to those working with traditional hand-drawn animation. Furthermore, as noted above, photorealistic CGI is now often indistinguishable from conventional live-action imagery. It is this technological capability that led Catmull to describe Pixar's 'Hyper-Reality' as 'a stylised realism that had a lifelike feel without actually being photorealistic' (Price 2008, 213). Pixar's hyper-realism, therefore, is a self-regulated mediation of the 'real', something to which Disney's animator's of the 1930s and 1940s could only aspire.

Charting the development of Pixar's hyper-realist style reveals an artistic ideology that has remained largely unaltered since the production of *Toy Story*. Focusing on character animation, *Toy Story* provides an excellent example of the stylized realism to which Catmull refers. Although computer technology was sufficiently advanced by the time *Toy Story* went into production, enabling, in principle, geometrically accurate soldiers to be animated, Pixar's animators rejected this level of realism in favour of a more expressive representation. (The real life toy soldiers that *Toy*

Story's combatants are based on were commonly moulded using plastic, which, while providing a small amount of malleability, would have maintained a fixed pose.) As Pixar writer and director Pete Doctor notes, when it was suggested that the soldiers might 'lift their feet up and the base would kind of follow along like a shadow or something,' Lasseter is said to have replied, 'they've got to stay stuck down, you've got to embrace the . . . inherent limitations of these toys' (*The Disney–Pixar South Bank Show*, ITV, 11 Oct 2009). In response, the animators increased the range of physical motion available to the soldiers, while maintaining their recognizable appearance, thus endowing characters that might otherwise have been stiff and lifeless with personality.

Similar manipulation can be seen in *Toy Story*'s background animation. Unlike hand-drawn animation, where backgrounds served to establish a location while also containing those elements of the shot that did not require movement, Pixar created fully 3-D 'sets'. In addition to this 3-D space, models were created 'for every inanimate object that the characters pick up, touch, or ride in onscreen, as well as for nearly every structural and decorative feature of every environment the characters explore: lamps, tables, furniture, bed frames, hallways, staircases, whole buildings' (Lasseter and Daly 1995, 48). One noticeable benefit of having digitally modelled 3-D 'sets' is volumetric consistency, which, when using traditional hand-drawn animation, is a difficult quality to maintain through dynamic camera movements such as tracking and panning. Additionally, whereas a hand-drawn sequence of animation using the shot/reverse-shot convention would require an artist to draw both perspectives as accurately as possible, a similar sequence in CG animation would just require the layout artist or director to program in the 'camera' angle and check the resulting shot for continuity.

However, Pixar's animators did not always obey the laws of physics. Set modeller Damir Frkovic reveals how, in making the Pizza Planet location, he had to 'do some fiddling with the restaurant's proportions to keep them pleasingly spherical', manipulating 'its shape in ways impossible with an actual set' (Lasseter and Daly 1995, 87). Frkovic concedes: 'That big enormous neon 'Pizza Planet' sign on top of the rings would break right through the roof if you built it the way we show' (Lasseter and Daly 1995, 87). Furthermore, a close inspection of *Ratatouille* (2007) reveals a subtle example of squash-and-stretch animation. At full speed, when Linguini bursts into the kitchen, the doors, while opened with force, appear to maintain their rigidity. However, when replayed at a speed of 12fps (or less) the doors can be seen to buckle substantially. The exaggerated curvature of the doors seemingly contradicts the physical parameters that govern the 3-D model. This brief example of squash-and-stretch, if not simply the result of a programmed algorithm, must be the product of an animator's manipulation. Given the success of Pixar's films, viewers evidently enjoy *seeing* this particular brand of stylized realism.

Significantly, *Cars* (2006) reveals the limits to which Pixar has been able to push its hyper-realist aesthetic. While audiences have been able to adequately suspend their disbelief and embrace Pixar's talking toys, bugs, monsters, fish and rats, *Cars*, for many, proved an exception to this rule. Not only is it frequently cited as the least popular Pixar film in internet forums, its anthropomorphic cast also prompted criticism from mainstream commentators. In her review for the *New York Times*, Manohla Dargis writes: 'Welcome to Weirdsville, Cartoonland, where automobiles race – and rule – in a world that, save for a thicket of tall pines and an occasional scrubby bush, is freakishly absent of any organic matter. Here, even the bugs singeing their wings on the porch light look like itty-bitty Volkswagen beetles' (2006). Dargis's renaming of Radiator Springs as 'Weirdsville' suggests a degree of unease in her engagement with the film, one which appears to centre around an inability to reconcile images of flying cars with Pixar's hyper-realism. The aesthetic choices made by Pixar on the production of *WALL-E (2008; discussed below)*, another film focusing on the life of a machine, suggests the studio was keen to ensure the film received a better reception than the one that greeted *Cars*.

An analysis of Pixar's box office performance between 1995 and 2010 (Figure 8.1) reveals the comparative 'failure' of *Cars*. Of the eleven films released by Pixar during this period, *Cars* recorded the third lowest worldwide gross; only *Toy Story* and *A Bug's Life*, Pixar's formative features, registered lower box office receipts.

Moreover, of the films released since 2001, when Pixar first recorded a gross in excess of $500 million, *Cars* has the second worst budget to gross ratio (a 384% return). *WALL-E* has the lowest budget to gross ratio (297%), although this may be partly due to the recession that was affecting the global economy at the time of the film's release. While arguably Pixar's weakest film to date, when placed in the broader context of mainstream film, *Cars* still represents a considerable commercial success.

Despite the importance of hyper-realism, certain aspects of Pixar's animation exhibit a more photorealist ethic. In *Monsters, Inc.*, not only did Pixar's animators attempt to legitimize the appearance of Sulley by having

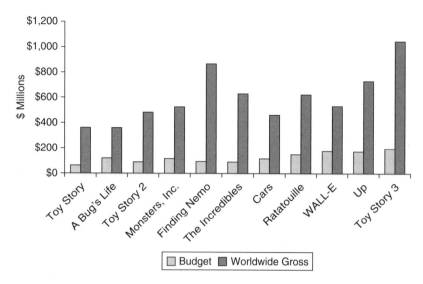

FIGURE 8.1 'Pixar – Budget/Gross Profile: First Run 1995–2010'

him echo the 'look and behaviour of a bear' (Wells 2009b, 112), they also undertook the task of producing realistic-looking fur. However, as Price observes, this posed several problems:

> [F]iguring out how to render the huge numbers of hairs – 2,320,413 on Sulley – in a reasonably efficient way. Another was making the hairs cast shadows on other hairs. Without self-shadowing, fur or hair takes on an unrealistic flat-coloured look. . . . Still another was giving the animators control over the direction and movement of the fur without imposing an inordinate burden on them. (2008, 199–200)

The answer was 'Fitz' (short for physics tool), a program which, through a series of inbuilt parameters, automated the simulation of fur, hair and cloth. If, after using Fitz, 'Sulley's fur was sticking up in an unattractive but technically accurate cowlick, the system . . . [afforded] the director and animators sufficient control to adjust the final image as needed' (Paik 2007, 197). In this instance, having come close to photorealistic fur, Pixar's animators once again ensured that their images would appear 'better than real' (Telotte 2008, 161).

Digital Disney

With a few exceptions, such as *Final Fantasy: The Spirits Within* (2001), *Final Fantasy VII: Advent Children* (2005) and 'Final Flight of the Osiris' from *The Animatrix* (2003), Pixar's hyper-realist aesthetic has become the industry standard, helping to shape Disney's digital aesthetic since *Dinosaur* (2000) – a film which was developed before Pixar effectively redefined the medium. For *Dinosaur,* the film's creative team 'sought to use the most up-to-date research about possible dinosaur skin colorization and the potential evolutionary relationship between dinosaurs and birds' (Wells 2009b, 92), in order to achieve a satisfactory level of authenticity. Following this, the opening forty-five seconds of Disney's subsequent CG feature, *Chicken Little* (2005), serve as a form of mission statement, self-reflexively drawing attention to the Studio's adoption of a more Pixar-like hyper-realism.

Chicken Little opens with a question: 'Where to begin?' How about, the narrator asks, 'Once Upon a Time?' At this point a ray of golden light fills the screen, prompting the 'camera' to tilt upward, following it to its source; however, just before the origin is reached, the light, along with the rising string music that had begun to swell, abruptly disappears, leaving only a black screen and the narrator's rhetorical statement: 'how many times have you heard that before, let's do something else' (*Chicken Little*). With renewed enthusiasm the narrator responds, 'I got it, I got it, here we go, here's how to open a movie' (*Chicken Little*). This prompts lyrical chanting and a sunrise scene, both of which clearly reference the opening of *The Lion King* (1994). Again, the narrator interjects, halting the introduction: 'No, I don't think so, it sounds familiar, doesn't it to you?' (*Chicken Little*). The final false start opens with an iris shot that reveals a leather storybook, which, accompanied by a pastoral piccolo acoustic, begins to open. The narrator interrupts for the last time: 'Oh no, not the book, how many times have you seen opening the book before? Close the book, we're not doing that' (*Chicken Little*). Finally, the narrator succeeds with his introduction and the film begins. We see a clock tower lit by a single shaft of sunlight, around which the 'camera' begins to spin; as the 'camera' revolves, getting closer with each pass, Chicken Little becomes visible at the tower's summit.

In addition to providing a humorous, self-referential introduction, the iconographic evocation of traditional Disney introductions and subsequent admission of their staleness serves to position *Chicken Little* as a film which, through an awareness of past Disney convention, could potentially offer something new and different. Secondly, the specificity of *The Lion King* reference can be seen as a comment on CG animation's usurpation of traditional 2-D animation. As noted in Chapter 6, upon its release *The Lion King* became the most successful animated feature of all time, grossing $783 worldwide; however, in 2003 *Finding Nemo* comfortably surpassed that mark, setting a new benchmark for animation with a worldwide gross of $864 million. Lastly, it appears as if Disney's digital animators are working from an artistic remit not dissimilar to that of traditional hand animators. When discussing the motivations behind his preference for animal characters, Chuck Jones once remarked: 'I am an animator and an animation director; therefore, I look for characters that cannot be done in live-action. That is what animation is all about; it is an extension beyond the ability of live-action motion pictures' (1990, 227). Whereas traditional hand animators, such as Jones, created characters, images and scenes, which could not be realized with live-action cinematography, Disney's digital animators introduce the eponymous Chicken Little with a 'camera' movement and lighting effect that would be difficult, but not impossible, to execute using traditional hand-drawn animation.

Through a comparison of two films released in 2008, *Bolt* and *WALL-E*, it is possible to see how Disney-branded computer animation still adheres to Pixar's hyper-realist principles, while also revealing how it has maintained the drive, evident as early as *Chicken Little*, to do something different. Beyond the visual differences necessitated by their respective storylines, the fundamentals of *Bolt* and *WALL-E*'s digital imagery remain relatively similar. Both animation teams would have worked within a 3-D environment, animated using 3-D character models, and would have had to wait until after the images had been rendered – the process that 'actualises the art' (Lasseter and Daly 1995, 168) – to see whether their finished animation worked on every level. Furthermore, on a mechanical level, *WALL-E* only marginally exceeds *Bolt* in its attention to detail, with both films seeking to replicate the effects lighting and camera lens choice have on real-world cinematography.

In live-action film, shooting into strong sunlight usually results in lens flare. Lens flare is the product of light entering the camera lens, causing 'rays to refract off of the many surfaces in the lens assembly' (Wright 2006, 208), which then strike the film and produce the flaring effect. Furthermore, as Ron Brinkmann observes, 'lens flare artifacts . . . are specific to the lens, not the light source. Because of this, they are always

FIGURE 8.2 Simulating lens flare in *WALL-E*.

the closest object to the camera. Nothing will ever pass in 'front' of a lens flare' (1999, 200). In *WALL-E* we see lens flare on a number of occasions, but it is most visible at 00:02:10 as WALL-E looks into the sun (Figure 8.2). In this frame we see a range of digitally composited lens flare effects, which give the impression of being 'caused' by the sun's brightness and the directness with which the 'camera' is orientated toward it. Although much subtler, *Bolt* features similar instances of lens flare. One example, when Bolt and Penny access a rooftop to spy on Dr Calico, sees the haze from a lighting source distort the upper right-hand corner of the image.

Another way in which both films attempt to replicate the qualities of live-action cinematography is through their manipulation of focus within close-ups. The close-up is one of the most expressive shots available to any filmmaker, especially when it is used to study a face (human or otherwise), as it can reveal the actor's subtle reactions and simulated microexpressions. Béla Balász argues that the facial expression is 'the most subjective manifestation of man', and that this 'most subjective and individual of human manifestations is rendered objective in the close-up' (2004, 316). Equally, the close-up, when featured as part of a sequence of shots, or montage, can help generate 'a sense of meaning not objectively contained in the images themselves but derived exclusively from their juxtaposition' (Bazin 2005, 25). However, a common feature of the close-up that is often neglected is the flattening of the shot's background through shallow focus. In live-action filmmaking, this effect can be the product of a number of things: an artistic choice on the part of the director,

FIGURES 8.3–8.4 (left to right) Manipulating background focus in *Bolt*.

or cinematographer, or the background imagery being outside of the camera's focal point.

Again, because no actual cameras were used to film *Bolt* or *WALL-E*, the presence of any out of focus imagery is the result of a creative decision. Interestingly, the close-ups featured in the opening few minutes of *Bolt* contain both focused and out of focus backgrounds (Figures 8.3 and 8.4). When we see Bolt and Penny on the rooftop in Figure 8.3, the focused background helps to quickly situate the pair topographically, reinforcing the distance between her and her father. Contrastingly, when the 'camera' zooms in on Bolt in Figure 8.4, not only does the foreground subject grow in prominence due to minor distortion (imitating what would have happened had a wide-angle lens been used to capture this shot), but the background falls out of focus, highlighting that it is up to the canine hero to save the day.

Focus is used more overtly in *WALL-E* as a way of controlling the viewer's gaze. As Bruce F. Kawin notes, 'the eye naturally gravitates towards objects that are in focus' and therefore 'the control of focus is a crucial aesthetic device' (1992, 137). This is clearly evident in Figures 8.5 and 8.6, in which we see the focus shift from the desolate background to a medium close-up of WALL-E.

In the context of the film, this shot helps to establish the scale of WALL-E's task, first presenting the sprawling urban wasteland, then reducing it to a singular, out of focus mass, which WALL-E alone must clear. Cinematographer Roger Deakins, who was briefly employed as a visual consultant on *WALL-E*, concludes:

> We discussed the use of lenses and how that . . . affects the three-dimensionality of the set, and allowing part of the set, as it were, to go dark, and allow something else to go very bright as a contrast to the

FIGURES 8.5–8.6   Shifting focus in *WALL-E*

very dark . . . I think it is wonderful the subtlety of the little focus shifts and using the idea of sources – lighting the set by choosing the sources you would put in it to give you the effect you want. You think, well, you don't really need to do that on an animated film, but it's those details that . . . the audience isn't consciously aware of [that] . . . sells the whole believability of it. (*WALL-E*, 'The Imperfect Lens Special Feature', 2008)

Whereas the opening ten minutes of *WALL-E* favours conservative cinematography (even the debris towers, presented from a bird's-eye view, echo the helicopter shots of Los Angeles featured in Michael Mann's *Collateral* [2004]), *Bolt* features a number shots that could not have been done in a live-action film. One example, between 00:03:20 and 00:03:28, sees the 'camera' track backwards, starting with a close-up of synaptic growth on a molecular level, and concluding with the 'camera' tracking out of Bolt's right eye before stopping in a close-up of his head. This movement relies on the principle of animated penetration, which concerns the 'visualisation of unimaginable psychological/physical/technical interiors' (Wells 2009a, 81). Additionally, the tracking shot (00:07:16–00:07:30), which sees Penny pulled by Bolt at high speed through busy traffic while being pursued by identikit henchmen, also exceeds what would be possible in live-action filmmaking.

On a macro level, both films reveal a desire to develop a subtle photo-realistic aesthetic. However, whereas *WALL-E* offers a continuation of Pixar's commitment to the creation of believable and 'recognisable' worlds through classically influenced cinematography, Disney's *Bolt* frequently foregrounds its technological virtuosity. It is this tendency towards eye-catching 'camerawork' that marks an area in which Disney's CG features are pulling away from Pixar's principles of hyper-realism and conventional cinematography.

Conclusion

The synthesis of Disney and Pixar has had a tremendous impact on both studios, although the most significant artistic result of this partnership only recently received a public release. Not only did *The Princess and the Frog* (2009) constitute a return by Disney to a 2-D hyperrealist aesthetic, the film also brought together the talents of Disney's most prolific – and arguably most important – Renaissance directors with serial Pixar composer Randy Newman (*Toy Story, A Bug's Life, Toy Story 2, Monsters, Inc.* and *Cars*), all under the stewardship of producer Peter Del Vecho (a long-time Disney employee) and executive producer Lasseter. However, had it not been for Lasseter, this return to a more traditional style of animation may have never happened.

Lasseter, from his earliest days at Pixar, was always keen to facilitate the artistic ambitions of his colleagues; so, when Clements and Musker brought their concept for *The Princess and the Frog* to him, he did not try to turn their idea into a CG project. Lasseter, speaking shortly after *The Princess and the Frog* was announced, stated:

> Aside from being long-time friends and colleagues, John and Ron are two of the most influential and imaginative filmmakers in the animation medium, and I am so excited to be working with them in bringing *their* creative vision . . . to the big screen. *They've* come up with an original story that is deeply rooted in the fairy tale tradition, and it's filled with great humour, emotion and musical moments. (Desowitz 2007)

Of this magnanimity Musker observes, 'John [Lasseter] loves 2-D. He wants to aim high, be timeless, raise the bar . . . John embraces Disney. He's not negative, like the last regime. He believes that quality will win out and that problems can be fixed' (Desowitz 2007).

Lasseter once remarked, it is 'because of the films of Walt Disney and the magical art form that [he] . . . helped create' that he decided to become an animator, and, 'if there's a studio in the world that should still be doing hand-drawn animation it should be the Walt Disney Animation Studio – the studio that started it all' (*The Princess and the Frog – The Return to Hand Drawn Animation*, 2009). Given the demand established by Pixar for CG animation, it is arguably *only* Disney that is now able to produce a 2-D animated feature capable of successfully competing in this market.

Conclusion – Happily Ever After?

The landscape of cinema has changed a great deal since Disney was a tenant of 'Poverty Row' during Hollywood's studio era. In the years since Disney helped fight against the major studios' stranglehold over film production, distribution and exhibition, the Disney Corporation itself has become part of the media industry's ruling class. It is for this reason that, more than ever, discussions of Disney animation must make every effort to separate fact from fiction. At the time of writing, Disney animation stands at a crossroads, with several factors promising to shape the Company's strategic development in the coming years.

With the films *The Princess and the Frog* (2009), *Tangled* (2010), *Winnie the Pooh* (2011) and the upcoming *Reboot Ralph* (2013), it appears that Disney has settled into a routine that will see the Studio alternate between hand-drawn and CG productions for the foreseeable future. While this might be a predictable and conservative strategy, catering to those audience members raised with CG animation, yet also intermittently offering something for the cinema-goers wanting something more traditional in appearance, there are very different creative ideologies underlying these two styles of feature. As noted in Chapter 7, with *The Princess and the Frog* exhibiting a primarily Disney-Formalist aesthetic, the Studio effectively signalled a return to the ethos of its Renaissance period, while at the same time distancing itself from the overt stylistic and structural experimentation of the Neo-Disney features. Consequently, *The Princess and the Frog* re-established a sense of continuity between how Disney hand-drawn animation has been traditionally perceived and how it exists today. *Winnie the Pooh*, although stylistically different to *The Princess and the Frog*, exhibits a similar emphasis on renewal. Contrastingly, Disney's CG features reveal the influence of outside forces – namely the features produced by DreamWorks Animation and Blue Sky Studios. With Pixar consistently pushing the envelope in its features (engaging, for example, with eco-politics in *WALL-E* [2008] and tackling themes such as miscarriage, bereavement and ageism in a heavy-hitting opening ten minutes in *Up* [2009]), those features released solely under the 'Disney' brand, while superficially appealing, feel conservative, if not tame, by comparison. Given the definite artistic impetus driving the Studio's hand-drawn animation, it is Disney's CG features which, in the face of strong competition, must now work hardest to reveal a worthwhile *raison d'être*.

Disney's traditional hand-drawn animation also faces a challenge though, albeit a potentially indirect one. On 31 August 2009, Disney announced that it had 'agreed to buy Marvel Entertainment for $4 billion', in what was described as 'the biggest media deal of the year' (Thomasch and Keating 2009). Although this figure may appear excessive, considering the recent economic instability and financial uncertainty, the deal has the potential to expand the Disney brand in areas that it considers to be underdeveloped. As a brand, Disney appeals to certain demographics more strongly than others. Mothers and daughters are perhaps the most prolific consumers, buying into synergized Disney commodities such as the Studio's Princess products (costumes, dolls and DVD/Blu-ray tie-ins, for example) and the *Hannah Montana* and *High School Musical* brands. Currently, however, young boys are considered the most lucrative demographic. Tom Lowry and Ronald Grover write: 'The U.S. has 30 million males aged 5 to 19, and capturing their attention with a TV show, movie, or magazine article is a boon to advertisers. Boys (or their parental proxies) are ravenous consumers who spend billions each year on apparel, toys, and video games' (2009). Therefore, the Marvel deal has the potential to attract more boys, thus 'balancing out Disney's big following among girls' (Lowry and Grover 2009). Marvel luminary Stan Lee also sees the upcoming deal as mutually beneficial, arguing that nobody produces or markets 'franchises better than Disney, and nobody has the extensive library of characters that would make great franchises that Marvel has' (Avila 2009).

Disney's Marvel investment can be seen to consolidate the business strategy that motivated the 2006 purchase of Pixar. In keeping with other aspects of the Corporation, it appears that Disney is keen to further diversify its animation in an attempt to appeal to the widest possible market. However, unlike the Pixar acquisition, which brought a lean and highly profitable enterprise under the Disney banner, Disney will have to do much of the work if it is to successfully 'mine' the characters in the Marvel 'treasure trove' (Foley 2009). Furthermore, if Disney chooses to develop any of the Marvel characters in an animated form, the Studio's own traditional animation, given the direct competition posed by such a development and by Pixar's CG animation, would need to ensure it returned adequate financial rewards. Such economic pressures, should they arise, would clearly problematize an extended return to the costly Disney-Formalist mode of filmmaking typified by *The Princess and the Frog*.

The greatest challenge now facing the Studio's traditional animation, however, is a development which has the potential to redefine the cinema-going experience itself: the proliferation of, and demand for, 3-D exhibition. Although not a new concept, Hollywood has recently turned to this method of presentation to combat the increasing appeal of the high-definition and on-demand home viewing experiences that are now readily available.

Despite enthusiastic promotion during the 1950s, Hollywood's experimentation with 3-D exhibition proved unsuccessful. This was primarily due to three key problems with the process: 'First, they were based upon routine genres or banal stories without properly developed characters. Second, viewers had to wear polarized glasses to see the stereoscopic 3-D effect. Third, they overused various cinematic tricks and gimmicks that assaulted the audience, sensationalising the film narrative' (Gazetas 2008, 181). While these issues stemmed from the specificities of 3-D production, such as the need to capture the profilmic event with two, simultaneously recording cameras and then interlace the images upon projection, contemporary 3-D processes are far less restrictive.

Production of 3-D films has accelerated rapidly in the past few years, with three features receiving a wide release in 2007, six in 2008, and seventeen in 2009. Given the growing feasibility, profitability and appeal of 3-D cinema, it is likely that Disney Digital 3-D will play an increasingly pivotal role in the Studio's future production and exhibition plans. So far, Disney Digital 3-D has been employed to bring depth to CG Disney and Disney–Pixar productions, such as *Up* (2009), *Toy Story* (3-D re-release, 2009), *Toy Story 2* (3-D re-release, 2009), *Toy Story 3* (2010) and *Tangled* (2010). In the future though, 3-D could provide the means for Disney to step back from the deep canvas and create a fully immersive 3-D environment with traditional 2-D animation; doing so could represent the culmination of what has been a seventy-year pursuit of animated realism.

In this regard, Pixar, with the short *Night & Day* (2010), has already demonstrated one way that this can be achieved. Following the encounter of the animated characters Night and Day, both of which exhibit clear 2-D squash-and-stretch physics, the short quickly establishes a shared sense of curiosity as both begin to perceive an aesthetic difference that sets them apart from each other: Day's body is filled with daytime imagery, while Night's body contains nocturnal imagery. This initial curiosity quickly gives way to mutual feelings of mistrust and xenophobia, predicated on their perceived difference, leading Night and Day to fight with each other. Fortunately, after this period of conflict, they both come to realize that each other's differences can actually provide a fresh, and often thrilling, perspective on subjects with which they believed they were already familiar. A good example of this occurs when Day boastfully shows the Las Vegas strip to Night, only for Night to swap positions with him to reveal the neon spectacle of Las Vegas after dark. After hearing a radio broadcast promoting a message of tolerance and inclusivity, Night and Day conclude the short by embracing one another. As the sun begins to rise/set, this provides a moment of visual unification, after which their appearances become inverted, with Day becoming Night and vice versa. Clearly, this short is intended to stress the importance of diversity, tolerance and cultural exchange in combating social disintegration – a concern shared globally. Because this short is animated, and therefore symbolically metamorphic by nature, Night and Day support various interpretations related to identity politics (such as ethnicity, gender, race and sexuality); however, it is the aesthetic significance of the short – its technological composition – that shall remain the focus here.

By framing the 3-D bodies of Night and Day with a 2-D animated outline, Pixar literally provides a window on how these two styles of animation can be successfully combined. While 3-D provides much of the spectacle in the short, it is the 2-D 'overlay' which determines what the spectator is able to see, thus shaping the narrative of diversity and reconciliation. While hand-drawn 2-D animation may not currently be able to compete with the popularity of its CG 3-D counterpart, it remains a hugely significant part of the history and language of animation as an art form. How it is to be used and developed now, in the face of this competition, is critical. Whereas television and online markets have witnessed a recent boom in 2-D animated shorts, it remains to be seen whether Disney is able to achieve a similar rebirth within the domain of feature film. Whatever the outcome, with regard to future creativity, the next few years promise to be a defining period in the ongoing evolution of Disney's traditional animation.

Works Cited

Adams, Mark, Eric Miller and Max Sims. (2004), *Inside Maya 5*. Indianapolis: New Riders.

Ades, Dawn. (1990), *Dalí*. London: Thames and Hudson.

Alberge, Dalya. (2007), 'Disney-Dalí premiere is 60 years late.' *The Times*, 19 January.

Alger, Dean. (1998), *Megamedia: How Giant Corporations Dominate Mass Media, Distort Competition, and Endanger Democracy*. Lanham: Rowman and Littlefield.

Anon. (2002), *Production Notes: Bringing the Character's to Life*. http://www.mooviees.com/325/683-production_notes (accessed January 30, 2010).

Anon. (2008), *Walt Disney Animation Studios, The Archive Series: Story*. New York: Disney.

Apodaca, Anthony A., and Larry Gritz. (1999), *Advanced RenderMan: Creating CGI for Motion Pictures*. San Diego: Academic.

Austin, Thomas, and Martin Barker. (2003), *Contemporary Hollywood Stardom*. London: Arnold.

Avila, Michael. (2009), 'Stan Lee sees Disney-Marvel as a Super Deal.' *msnbc*. 1 September. http://www.msnbc.msn.com/id/32645353/ns/business-media_biz/ (accessed September 9, 2010).

'Awards for Fantasia.' *The Internet Movie Database*. http://www.imdb.com/title/tt0032455/awards (accessed 9 September 2010).

Balász, Béla. (2004), 'The Close-Up.' In *Film Theory and Criticism*, edited by Leo Braudy and Marshall Cohen, 304–11. Oxford: Oxford University Press.

Barker, Martin. (2003), 'Introduction.' In *Contemporary Hollywood Stardom*, edited by Thomas Austin and Martin Barker, 1–24. London: Arnold.

Barrier, Michael. (1999), *Hollywood Cartoons: American Animation in its Golden Age*. Oxford: Oxford University Press.

—. (2008), *The Animated Man: A Life of Walt Disney*. Berkeley: University of California Press.

Barthes, Roland. (1975), *The Pleasure of the Text*. New York: Hill and Wang.

—. (1995), 'The Death of the Author.' In *Authorship From Plato to the Postmodern*, edited by Sean Burke, 125–30. Edinburgh: Edinburgh University Press.

Bazin, André. (2005), 'The Evolution of the Language of Cinema.' In *What is Cinema? Volume 1*, translated by Hugh Gray, 23–41. Berkeley: University of California Press.

Beck, Jerry. (2004), *Animation Art: From Pencil to Pixel, the History of Cartoon, Anime, and CGI*. London: Flame Tree.

—. (2005), *The Animated Movie Guide*. Chicago: A Cappella.

'Board of Directors.' *The Walt Disney Company: Corporate Information.* http://corpo-rate.disney.go.com/corporate/bios/robert_a_iger.html (accessed 31 August 2010).

Boje, David M. (1995), 'Stories of the Storytelling Organization: A postmodern analysis of Disney as 'Tamara-Land'.' *Academy of Management Journal* 38: 997–1035.

Bordwell, David, and Kristin Thompson. (2001), *Film Art: An Introduction.* New York: McGraw-Hill.

Bosquet, Alain. (2003), *Conversations with Dalí.* Translated by Joachim Neugro-schel. New York: Ubu.

Botti, Timothy J. (2006), *Envy of the World: A History of the U.S. Economy and Big Business.* New York: Algora.

Breton, André. (1934), *What is Surrealism? A lecture given at a meeting of the Belgian Surrealists (Brussels).* 1 June. http://home.wlv.ac.uk/~fa1871/whatsurr.html (accessed 10 August 2010).

—. (1969), *Manifestoes of Surrealism.* Translated by Richard Seaver and Helen R. Lane. Ann Arbor, MI: Michigan University Press.

—. (1972), 'Le Cas Dalí.' In *Surrealism and Painting,* translated by Simon Watson Taylor, 130–5. London: Macdonald.

Brewster, Percy D. (1917), *Film For Color Cinematography.* United States Patent 1222925. 17 April.

Brinkmann, Ron. (1999), *The Art and Science of Digital Compositing.* San Diego: Academic.

Browder, Clifford. (1967), *André Breton: Arbiter of Surrealism.* Genève: Libairie Droz.

Bryman, Alan. (1995), *Disney and His Worlds.* London: Routledge.

—. (1997), 'Animating the Pioneer Versus Late Entrant Debate: An Historical Case Study.' *Journal of Management Studies* 34, no. 3: 415–38.

Burlingame, Jon. (2000), *Sound and Vision: 60 Years of Motion Picture Soundtracks.* New York: Billboard.

Byrne, Eleanor, and Martin McQuillan. (1999), *Deconstructing Disney.* London: Pluto.

Campbell, Joseph. (1993), *The Hero with a Thousand Faces.* London: HarperCol-lins. First published: 1949.

Canemaker, John. (1994), 'Life Before Mickey.' *The New York Times,* 10 July.

—. (1996), *Before the Animation Begins: The Art and Lives of Disney Inspirational Sketch Artists.* New York: Hyperion.

—. (1999), *Paper Dreams: The Art And Artists Of Disney Storyboards.* New York: Disney.

—. (2001), *Walt Disney's Nine Old Men and the Art of Animation.* New York: Disney Editions.

Clements, Ron, and Ted Elliot. (1991), *Aladdin.* London: Hollywood Scripts.

Cook, David A. (2004), *A History of Narrative Film.* New York: Norton.

Cotterell, Arthur. (1986), *A Dictionary of World Mythology.* Oxford: Oxford Univer-sity Press.

Cowen, Ron. (1998), 'George Gershwin: He Got Rhythm.' *Washington Post,* 11 November.

Crawford, Alison. (2009), ' "Oh Yeah!": Family Guy as Magical Realism?' *Journal of Film and Video* 61, no. 2: 52–69.

Culhane, John. (1983), *Walt Disney's Fantasia*. New York: Harry N. Abrams.

—. (1999), *Fantasia 2000: Visions of Hope*. New York: Disney.

Dargis, Manohla. (2006), ' "Cars" Is a Drive Down a Lonely Highway.' *New York Times*, 9 June.

Davis, Amy M. (2006), *Good Girls and Wicked Witches: Women in Disney's Feature Animation*. London: John Libbey.

Davison, Annette. (2004), *Hollywood Theory, Non-Hollywood Practice*. Aldershot: Ashgate.

Dean, Carolyn J. (2001), 'History, Pornography and the Social Body.' In *Surrealism: Desire Unbound*, edited by Jennifer Mundy, 227–44. London: Tate.

Desowitz, Bill. (2003a), *Disney/Dali's Completed Destino Kicks Off Annecy Fest*. http://www.awn.com/articles/disneydalis-completed-idestinoi-kicks-annecy-fest (accessed 24 May 2010).

—. (2003b), *Hench Discusses Legendary Link to Dali and Disney on Destino*. 16 October. http://www.awn.com/articles/hench-discusses-legendary-link-dali-and-disney-idestinoi (accessed 26 July 2010).

—. (2007), 'Disney Greenlights 2-D The Frog Princess.' *Animation World Magazine*. 8 March. http://www.awn.com/news/films/disney-greenlights-2-D-frog-princess (accessed 1 September 2010).

Disney Miller, Diane. (1956), *The Story of Walt Disney*. New York: Dell.

Disney, Roy E. (2003), 'Letter of Resignation.' *USAToday.com*. 30 November. http://www.usatoday.com/money/media/2003–12–01-disney-letter_x.htm.

Dovey, Jon, Seth Giddings, Iain Grant, Kieran Kelly and Martin Lister. (2009), *New Media: A Critical Introduction*. London: Routledge.

Drees, Rich. 'Who Delayed Roger Rabbit?' *FilmBuffOnline*. http://www.film-buffonline.com/Features/RogerRabbitII.2.htm (accessed 14 August 2010).

Duchovnay, Gerald. (2004), 'Don Bluth.' In *Film Voices: Interviews from Post Script*, edited by Gerald Duchovnay, 143–52. New York: State University of New York Press.

Dyer, Richard. (1999), *Stars*. London: BFI.

—. (2004), *Heavenly Bodies: Film Stars and Society*. London: Routledge.

Eisen, Armand. (1975), 'Two Disney Artists.' *Crimmer's: The Harvard Journal of Pictorial Fiction*, Winter: 35–44.

Eisenstein, Sergei. (1986), *Eisenstein on Disney*. Edited by Jay Leyda. Translated by Alan Upchurch. London: Methuen.

Eisner, Michael. (1999), *Work in Progress: Risking Failure, Surviving Success*. New York: Hyperion.

Eliot, Marc. (2003), *Walt Disney: Hollywood's Dark Prince*. London: André Deutsch.

Eller, Claudia, and Richard Verrier. (2004), 'A Clash of CEO Egos Gets Blame in Disney-Pixar Split.' *Los Angeles Times*, 2 February.

Emmeche, Claus. (1994), *The Garden in the Machine: The Emerging Science of Artificial Life*. Princeton: Princeton University Press.

Fabrikant, Geraldine. (1988), 'The Media Business: Advertising; Marketing Movies for Children.' *The New York Times.* 28 November. http://query.nytimes. com/gst/fullpage.html?res=940DE1D7133AF93BA15752C1A96E948260 (accessed 26 August 2010).

Finch, Christopher. (1995a), *The Art of The Lion King.* New York: Hyperion.

—. (1995b), *The Art of Walt Disney: from Mickey Mouse to the Magic Kingdoms.* New York: Harry N. Abrams.

Finkelstein, Haim. (1996), 'Dali and Un Chien andalou: The Nature of a Collaboration.' In *Dada and Surrealist Film,* edited by Rudolf E. Kuenzli, 128–42. Cambridge: MIT.

—. (2004), 'Dalí's Small Stage of Paranoiac Ceremonial.' In *Companion to Spanish Surrealism,* edited by Robert Havard, 117–40. Woodbridge: Tamesis.

Fleischer, Max. (1936), *Art of Making Motion Picture Cartoons.* United States Patent 2054414. 15 September.

Fleischer, Richard. (2005), *Out of the Inkwell: Max Fleischer and the Animation Revolution.* Kentucky: University Press of Kentucky.

Foley, Stephen. (2009), 'Disney Ups Testosterone with $4bn Marvel Deal.' *The Independent,* 1 September.

Ford, Larry R. (1994), *Cities and Buildings: Skyscrapers, Skid Rows, and Suburbs.* Baltimore: The John Hopkins University Press.

Frayling, Christopher, Bob Godfrey, Zack Schwartz and Paul Wells. (1997), 'Disney Discourse: On Caricature, Conscience Figures and Mickey Too.' In *Art and Animation,* edited by Paul Wells, 4–9. London: Academy.

Freud, Sigmund. (1950), *The Ego and the Id.* Translated by Joan Riviere. London: Hogarth Press.

Friedman, Lester D. (2006), *Citizen Spielberg.* Urbana: University of Illinois Press.

Furniss, Maureen. (2007), *Art in Motion: Animation Aesthetics.* London: John Libbey.

Gabler, Neal. (2006), *Walt Disney: The Triumph of the American Imagination.* New York: Alfred A. Knopf.

Garity, William E., and John N. A. Hawkins. (1940), *Sound Reproducing System.* United States of America Patent 2298618. 31 July.

Gazetas, Aristides. (2008), *An Introduction to World Cinema.* Jefferson: McFarland.

Giroux, Henry A. (2001), *The Mouse that Roared.* Lanham, MD: Rowman and Littlefield.

Gomery, Douglas. (1994), 'Disney's Business History.' In *Disney Discourse: Producing the Magic Kingdom,* edited by Eric Smoodin, 71–86. London: Routledge.

Govil, Nitin. (2005), 'Hollywood's Effects, Bollywood FX.' In *Contracting Out Hollywood: Runaway Productions and Foreign Location Shooting,* edited by Greg Elmer and Mike Gasher, 92–114. Lanham, MD: Rowman and Littlefield.

Gray, Jonathan. (2005), 'Television Teaching: Parody, The Simpsons, and Media Literacy Education.' *Critical Studies in Media Communication* 22: 223–38.

Griffin, Sean. (2000), *Tinker Belles and Evil Queens: the Walt Disney Company from the Inside Out.* New York: New York University Press.

Gritten, David. (2009), 'Bolt – Interview with director John Lasseter.' *Telegraph,* 4 March.

Hahn, Don. (1996), *Animation Magic*. New York: Disney.

Hall, Thomas Emerson, and J. David Ferguson. (1998), *The Great Depression: An International Disaster of Perverse Economic Policies*. Ann Arbor, MI: University of Michigan Press.

Handzo, Stephen. (1985), 'A Narrative Glossary of Film Sound Technology.' In *Theory and Practice: Film Sound*, edited by Elisabeth Weis and John Belton, 383–426. New York: Columbia University Press.

Happé, L. Bernard. (1971), *Basic Motion Picture Technology*. London: Focal.

Harbord, Janet. (2007), *The Evolution of Film: Rethinking Film Studies*. Cambridge: Polity.

Harris, Thomas L. (1998), *Value-Added Public Relations*. Chicago: McGraw-Hill.

Harris-Warrick, Rebecca. (1986), 'Ballroom Dancing at the Court of Louis XIV.' *Early Music* 14: 41–50.

Holliss, Richard, and Brian Sibley. (1988), *The Disney Studio Story*. London: Octopus.

Holson, Laura. (2004), 'Pixar to Find Its Own Way as Disney Partnership Ends.' *New York Times*. 31 January.

—. (2006), 'Disney Agrees to Acquire Pixar in a $7.4 Billion Deal.' *New York Times*, 25 January.

Iwerks, Leslie, and John Kenworthy. (2001), *The Hand Behind the Mouse*. New York: Disney.

Jackson, Kathi. (2007), *Steven Spielberg: A Biography*. Westport: Greenwood.

Jones, Chuck. (1990), *Chuck Amuck*. London: Simon and Schuster.

Kawin, Bruce F. (1992), *How Movies Work*. Berkeley: University of California Press.

Kerlow, Isaac V. (2004), *The Art of 3-D Computer Animation and Effects*. New York: John Wiley and Sons.

King, Geoff, and Tanya Krzywinska. (2000), *Science Fiction Cinema: From Outerspace to Cyberspace*. London: Wallflower.

Knowlton, Christopher. (1989), 'How Disney Keeps the Magic Going.' *Fortune Magazine*. 4 December. http://money.cnn.com/magazines/fortune/fortune_archive/1989/12/04/72827/index.htm (accessed 7 August 2010).

Koepp, Stephen. (1988), 'Do You Believe in Magic?' *Time Magazine*. 25 April. http://www.time.com/time/magazine/article/0,9171,967226–2,00.html (accessed 25 August 2010).

Kurtti, Jeff. (1998), *The Art of Mulan*. New York: Hyperion.

—. (2002), *Treasure Planet: A Voyage of Discovery*. New York: Disney.

—. (2009), *The Art of The Princess and the Frog*. San Francisco: Chronicle.

Langer, Mark. (1990), 'Regionalism in Disney Animation: Pink Elephants and Dumbo.' *Film History* 4: 305–21.

Lasseter, John, and Steve Daly. (1995), *Toy Story: The Art and Making of the Animated Film*. New York: Hyperion.

Lenburg, Jeff. (2006), *Who's Who in Animated Cartoons*. New York: Applause.

Leslie, Esther. (2004), *Hollywood Flatlands: Animation, Critical Theory and the Avant-Garde*. London: Verso.

Letter To Shareholders. (1999), Annual Report, The Walt Disney Company.

Lewis, Jon. (1994), 'Disney after Disney: Family Business and the Business of Family.' In *Disney Discourse Producing the Magic Kingdom*, edited by Eric Smoodin, 87–105. London: Routledge.

Linzmayer, Owen W. (2004), *Apple Confidential 2.0: The Definitive History of the World's Most Colourful Company*. San Francisco: William Pollock.

Lionel. (2009), 'Reitherman Reruns.' *Mayerson on Animation: Reflections on the Art and Business of Animation*. 18 March. http://mayersononanimation.blogspot.com/2009/03/reitherman-reruns.html (accessed 7 September 2010).

Lowry, Tom, and Ronald Grover. (2009), 'Disney's Marvel Deal and the Pursuit of Boys.' *BusinessWeek*. 10 September. http://www.businessweek.com/magazine/content/09_38/b4147066139865.htm (accessed 9 September 2010).

Mallan, Kerry, and Roderick McGillis. (2005), 'Between a Frock and a Hard Place: Camp Aesthetics and Children's Culture.' *Canadian Review of American Studies* 35: 1–19.

Maltby, Richard. (2003), *Hollywood Cinema*. Malden: Blackwell.

Maltin, Leonard. (1973), *The Disney Films*. New York: Crown.

—. (1987), *Of Mice and Magic: A History of American Animated Cartoons*. New York: Plume.

McBride, Joseph. (2006), *What Ever Happened to Orson Welles?* Lexington: University Press of Kentucky.

McCarthy, Helen. (1993), *Anime! A Beginner's Guide to Japanese Animation*. London: Titan.

McDonald, Paul. (2000), *The Star System: Hollywood's Production of Popular Identities*. London: Wallflower.

Mori, Masahiro. (1970), 'The Uncanny Valley.' *Energy* 7, no. 4: 33–5.

Neupert, Richard. (1994), 'Painting a Plausible World: Disney's Color Prototypes.' In *Disney Discourse: Producing the Magic Kingdom*, by Eric Smoodin, 106–17. London: Routledge.

Norman, Floyd. (2009), 'Reitherman Reruns.' *Mayerson on Animation: Reflections on the Art and Business of Animation*. 20 March. http://mayersononanimation.blogspot.com/2009/03/reitherman-reruns.html (accessed 7 September 2010).

Paik, Karen. (2007), *To Infinity and Beyond: The Story of Pixar Animation Studios*. London: Virgin.

Pat. (2009), 'Reitherman Reruns.' *Mayerson on Animation: Reflections on the Art and Business of Animation*. 18 March. http://mayersononanimation.blogspot.com/2009/03/reitherman-reruns.html (accessed 7 September 2010).

Perisic, Zoran. (2000), *Visual Effects Cinematography*. Woburn: Focal.

Philips, Mark. (2001), 'Summary of the Project – The Global Disney Audiences Project: Disney across Cultures.' In *Dazzled by Disney: The Global Disney Audiences Project*, edited by Janet Wasko, Mark R. Philips and Eileen R. Meehan, 31–61. London: Continuum.

'Pixar Dumps Disney.' (2004), *CNN Money*. 30 January.

Postal, Leslie. (1996), 'Celebration School Schedule Gets Boost: Disney and District Officials Work Out a Payment to Avoid Postponing Construction.' *Orlando Sentinel*, 14 April: 1.

Pratt, Doug. (2004), *Doug Pratt's DVD: Vol 2*. New York: Harbor.

Prendergast, Roy M. (1991), *Film Music: A Neglected Art*. New York: Norton.

Price, David A. (2008), *The Pixar Touch: The Making of a Company*. New York: Alfred A. Knopf.

Propp, Vladimir. (1968), *Morphology of the Folktale*. Translated by Laurence Scott. Austin: University of Texas Press. First published: 1928.

Pruiksma, Dave. (2006), *A Happy Ending Seems Eminent*. February. http://www.pruiksma.com/A%20NOT%20So%20Silly%20Symphony.html (accessed 31 August, 2010).

Rebello, Stephen. (1997a), *The Art of Hercules: The Chaos of Creation*. New York: Hyperion.

—. (1997b), *The Art of the Hunchback of Notre Dame*. New York: Hyperion.

Redmond, Sean. (2009), 'Film Since 1980.' In *The Routledge Companion to Science Fiction*, edited by Mark Bould, Andrew M. Butler, Adam Roberts and Sherryl Vint, 134–43. London: Routledge.

Reynolds, Nigel. (2007), 'When Dali met Walt – it was just surreal.' *Telegraph*, 31 May.

Rink, John. 'Rhapsody.' (2001), In *The New Grove Dictionary of Music and Musicians*, edited by Stanley Sadie, 254–5. London: Grove.

Roos, Robert De. (1994), 'The Magical Worlds of Walt Disney.' In *Disney Discourse: Producing the Magic Kingdom*, edited by Eric Smoodin, 48–68. London: Routledge.

Rushe, Dominic. (2003), 'The Little Fish that Hooked Disney.' *The Sunday Times*, 31 August.

Schickel, Richard. (1997), *The Disney Version: The Life, Times, Art and Commerce of Walt Disney*. Chicago: Elephant.

Schumach, Murray. (1961), 'Film's by Disney Work Two Ways.' *New York Times*, 13 November.

Semaj. (2009), 'Reitherman Reruns.' *Mayerson on Animation: Reflections on the Art and Business of Animation*. 18 March. http://mayersononanimation.blogspot.com/2009/03/reitherman-reruns.html (accessed 7 September 2010).

Serota, Nicholas. (2001), 'Foreward.' In *Surrealism: Desire Unbound*, edited by Jennifer Mundy, 7–8. London: Tate Publishing.

Shifrin, Art. (1983), 'The Trouble with Kinetoscope.' *American Cinematographer* 64, no. 9: 50+.

Sito, Tom. (2006), *Drawing the Line: The Untold Story of the Animation Unions from Bosko to Bart Simpson*. Lexington: University Press of Kentucky.

Smith, Dave, and Steven Clark. (2002), *Disney: The First 100 Years*. New York: Disney Editions.

Smith, Dave. (2006), *Disney A–Z: The Official Encyclopaedia*. New York: Disney.

Sobchack, Vivian. (1998), *Screening Space: The American Science Fiction Film*. New Jersey: Rutgers Universtiy Press.

Solomon, Charles. (1994), *Enchanted Drawings: The History of Animation*. New York: Wings.

—. (1995), *The Disney that Never Was: The Stories and Art from Five Decades of Unproduced Animation*. New York: Hyperion.

Taylor, John. (1987), *Storming the Magic Kingdom: Wall Street, the Raiders and the Battle for Disney*. New York: Alfred A. Knopf.

Taylor, Richard. (2000), *The Battleship Potemkin*. London: I. B. Tauris.

Telotte, J. P. (2001), *Science Fiction Film*. Cambridge: Cambridge University Press.

—. (2002), 'The New Hollywood Musical: From Saturday Night Fever to Footloose.' In *Genre and Contemporary Hollywood*, edited by Steve Neale, 48–61. London: BFI.

—. (2006), 'Ub Iwerks' (Multi)Plain Cinema.' *Animation: An Interdisciplinary Journal* 1, no. 1: 9–24.

—. (2008), *The Mouse Machine: Disney and Technology*. Champaign: University of Illinois Press.

Tengler, Nancy. (2003), *New Era Value Investing: A Disciplined Approach to Buying Value and Growth Stocks*. New York: John Wiley and Sons.

Terzopoulos, Demetri, Xiaoyuan In and Kiran Joshi. (1998), 'Behavioural Modelling and Animation (Panel): Past, Present, and Future.' *International Conference on Computer Graphics and Interactive Techniques: ACM SIGGRAPH 98 Conference Abstracts and Applications*. 209–11.

Terzopoulos, Demetri. (1999), 'Artificial Life for Computer Graphics.' *Communications of the ACM* 42, no. 8: 32–42.

Thomas, Bob. (1994), *Walt Disney: An American Original*. New York: Disney Editions.

—. (1997), *Disney's Art of Animation from Mickey Mouse to Hercules*. New York: Hyperion.

Thomas, Frank, and Ollie Johnson. (1995), *The Illusion of Life: Disney Animation*. New York: Hyperion.

Thomasch, Paul, and Gina Keating. (2009), 'Disney to Acquire Marvel in $4 Billion Deal.' *Reuters*. 31 August. http://www.reuters.com/article/idUSN3143303120090831 (accessed 9 September 2010).

'Trivia for Aladdin.' *The Internet Movie Database*. http://www.imdb.com/title/tt0103639/trivia (accessed 2 September 2010).

Waldberg, Patrick. (1962), *Surrealism*. Translated by Stuart Gilbert. Cleveland: World Publishing.

Ward, Paul. (2006), 'Some Thoughts on Practice-Theory Relationships in Animation Studies.' *Animation: An Interdisciplinary Journal* 1: 229–45.

Wasko, Janet. (2001), *Understanding Disney: The Manufacture of Fantasy*. Oxford: Polity.

Wasser, Frederick. (2001), *Veni, Vidi, Video: The Hollywood Empire and the VCR*. Austin: University of Texas Press.

Watts, Steven. (1995), 'Walt Disney's Art and Politics in the American Century.' *The Journal of American History* 82: 84–110.

—. (1997), *The Magic Kingdom: Walt Disney and the American Way of Life*. Columbia: University of Missouri Press.

Wells, Paul. (1996), 'Tom and Jerry: cat suits and mouse-taken identities.' In *The Gendered Object*, edited by Pat Kirkham, 184–95. Manchester: Manchester University Press.

—. (1998), *Understanding Animation*. London: Routledge.

—. (2002a), *Animation and America*. Edinburgh: Edinburgh University Press.

—. (2002b), *Animation: Genre and Authorship*. London: Wallflower.

—. (2002c), ' "I Wanna be like you-oo-oo": Disneyfied politics and identity from Mermaid to Mulan.' In *American Film and Politics from Reagan to Bush Jr*, edited by Philip John Davies and Paul Wells, 139–54. Manchester: Manchester University Press.

—. (2006), *The Fundamentals of Animation*. Lausanne: AVA.

—. (2009a), *Basics Animation: Drawing for Animation*. Lausanne: AVA.

—. (2009b), *The Animated Bestiary: Animals, Cartoons, and Culture*. New Brunswick: Rutgers University Press.

Whitaker, Harold, and John Halas. (2002), *Timing For Animation*. Oxford: Focal.

White, Tony. (2006), *Animation: From Pencils to Pixels*. Oxford: Focal.

Williams, David R. (1987a), 'Extracts from Story Conference Notes Relating to Snow White and the Seven Dwarfs: Animators meeting supervised by Dave Hand (18 Feb, 1937).' In *Snow White and the Seven Dwarfs Special Collection*. London: British Film Institute National Archive.

—. (1987b), 'Extracts from Story Conference Notes Relating to Snow White and the Seven Dwarfs: Discussion of Snow White's personality (11 Nov, 1936).' In *Snow White and the Seven Dwarfs Special Collection*. London: British Film Institute National Archive.

—. (1987c), 'Extracts from Story Conference Notes Relating to Snow White and the Seven Dwarfs: Full meeting of animators (23 Feb, 1937).' In *Snow White and the Seven Dwarfs Special Collection*. London: British Film Institute National Archive.

—. (1987d), 'Extracts from Story Conference Notes Relating to Snow White and the Seven Dwarfs: The Dwarf's Personalities (6 Jan, 1936).' In *Snow White and the Seven Dwarfs Special Collection*. London: British Film Institute National Archive.

Williams, Richard. (2001), *The Animator's Survival Kit: A Manual of Methods, Principles and Formulas for Classical, Computer, Games, Stop Motion and Internet Animators*. London: Faber.

Wordsworth, William. (1984), 'Preface to the Lyrical Ballads (1802).' In *William Wordsworth: A Critical Edition of the Major Works*, edited by Stephen Gill, 595–615. Oxford: Oxford University Press.

Wright, Steve. (2006), *Digital Compositing for Film and Video*. Oxford: Focal.

Zipes, Jack. (1996), 'Breaking the Disney Spell.' In *From Mouse to Mermaid: The Politics of Film, Gender, and Culture*, edited by Elizabeth Bell, Lynda Hass and Laura Sells, 21–42. Indiana: Indiana University Press.

Filmography

For ease of reference, the Filmography is divided into two sections. Listed first are Disney's theatrically released animated features, the fifty animated features which, as noted in the Introduction, are identified on the 'History' page of the official *Walt Disney Animation Studios* website. Rather than list these films alphabetically, because they reflect a single-studio production history, they are arranged chronologically. The second section, named 'Other', alphabetically lists all remaining referenced 'filmic' sources. This final section includes feature animation, short animation, animation–live-action hybrids, live-action films and televisual material.

Disney's Animated Features

Snow White and the Seven Dwarfs (David Hand, 1937)

Pinocchio (Hamilton Luske and Ben Sharpsteen, 1940)

Fantasia (James Algar, Samuel Armstrong, Ford Beebe, Norman Ferguson, Jim Handley, T. Hee, Wilfred Jackson, Hamilton Luske, Bill Roberts, Paul Satterfield and Ben Sharpsteen, 1940)

Dumbo (Ben Sharpsteen, 1941)

Bambi (David Hand, 1942)

Saludos Amigos (Norman Ferguson, Wilfred Jackson, Jack Kinney, Hamilton Luske and Bill Roberts, 1943)

The Three Caballeros (Norman Ferguson, 1944)

Make Mine Music (Bob Cormack, Clyde Geronimi, Jack Kinney, Hamilton Luske and Joshua Meador, 1946)

Fun and Fancy Free (Jack Kinney, Hamilton Luske, Bill Roberts and William Morgan, 1947)

Melody Time (Clyde Geronimi, Wilfred Jackson, Jack Kinney and Hamilton Luske, 1948)

The Adventures of Ichabod and Mr. Toad (James Algar, Clyde Geronimi and Jack Kinney, 1949)

Cinderella (Clyde Geronimi, Wilfred Jackson and Hamilton Luske, 1950)

Alice in Wonderland (Clyde Geronimi, Wilfred Jackson and Hamilton Luske, 1951)

Peter Pan (Clyde Geronimi, Wilfred Jackson and Hamilton Luske, 1953)

Lady and the Tramp (Clyde Geronimi, Wilfred Jackson and Hamilton Luske, 1955)

Sleeping Beauty (Clyde Geronimi, 1959)
One Hundred and One Dalmatians (Clyde Geronimi, Hamilton Luske and Wolfgang Reitherman, 1961)
The Sword in the Stone (Wolfgang Reitherman, 1963)
The Jungle Book (Wolfgang Reitherman, 1967)
The Aristocats (Wolfgang Reitherman, 1970)
Robin Hood (Wolfgang Reitherman, 1973)
The Many Adventures of Winnie the Pooh (Wolfgang Reitherman and John Lounsbery, 1977)
The Rescuers (John Lounsbery, Wolfgang Reitherman and Art Stevens, 1977)
The Fox and the Hound (Ted Berman, Richard Rich and Art Stevens, 1981)
The Black Cauldron (Ted Berman and Richard Rich, 1985)
The Great Mouse Detective (Ron Clements, Burny Mattinson, David Michener and John Musker, 1986)
Oliver and Company (George Scribner, 1988)
The Little Mermaid (Ron Clements and John Musker, 1989)
The Rescuers Down Under (Hendel Butoy and Mike Gabriel, 1990)
Beauty and the Beast (Gary Trousdale and Kirk Wise, 1991)
Aladdin (Ron Clements and John Musker, 1992)
The Lion King (Roger Allers and Rob Minkoff, 1994)
Pocahontas (Mike Gabriel and Eric Goldberg, 1995)
The Hunchback of Notre Dame (Gary Trousdale and Kirk Wise, 1996)
Hercules (Ron Clements and John Musker, 1997)
Mulan (Tony Bancroft and Barry Cook, 1998)
Tarzan (Chris Buck and Kevin Lima, 1999)
Fantasia 2000 (James Algar, Gaëtan Brizzi, Paul Brizzi, Hendel Butoy, Francis Glebas, Eric Goldberg, Don Hahn and Pixote Hunt, 1999)
Dinosaur (Eric Leighton and Ralph Zondag, 2000)
The Emperor's New Groove (Mark Dindal, 2000)
Atlantis: The Lost Empire (Gary Trousdale and Kirk Wise, 2001)
Lilo and Stitch (Dean DeBlois and Chris Sanders, 2002)
Treasure Planet (Ron Clements and John Musker, 2002)
Brother Bear (Aaron Blaise and Robert Walker, 2003)
Home on the Range (Will Finn and John Sanford, 2004)
Chicken Little (Mark Dindal, 2005)
Meet the Robinsons (Stephen J. Anderson, 2007)
Bolt (Byron Howard and Chris Williams, 2008)
The Princess and the Frog (Ron Clements and John Musker, 2009)
Tangled (Nathan Greno and Byron Howard, 2010)

Other

2001: A Space Odyssey (Stanley Kubrick, 1968)
Ace Ventura: When Nature Calls (Steve Oedekerk, 1995)
Adventures of Prince Achmed, The (Lotte Reiniger, 1926)
Adventures of Robin Hood, The (Michael Curtiz and William Keighley, 1938)

Akira (Katsuhiro Ôtomo, 1988)
Alice Comedies (Series: Laugh-O-Gram Films/Walt Disney Productions, 1923–27)
American Tail, An (Don Bluth, 1986)
Anastasia (Don Bluth and Gary Goldman, 1997)
Animatrix, The (Peter Chung, Andy Jones, Yoshiaki Kawajiri, Takeshi Koike, Mahiro Maeda, Kôji Morimoto and Shinichirô Watanabe, 2003)
Babe (Chris Noonan, 1995)
Batman Returns (Tim Burton, 1992)
Bedknobs and Broomsticks (Robert Stevenson, 1971)
Belle's Magical World (Cullen Blaine, Dale Case, Daniel de la Vega, Barbara Dourmashkin, Bob Kline, Burt Medall and Mitch Rochon, 1998)
Belle's Tales of Friendship (Jimbo Marshall, 1999)
Betty Boop (Series: Fleischer Studios, 1930–39)
Black Hole, The (Gary Nelson, 1979)
Blade Runner (Ridley Scott, 1982)
Brian Does Hollywood (Gavin Dell, 2001)
Bug's Life, A (John Lasseter and Andrew Stanton, 1998)
Cars (John Lasseter and Joe Ranft, 2006)
Cartoon Wars Part I (Trey Parker, 2006)
Cartoon Wars Part II (Trey Parker, 2006)
Casper (Brad Silberling, 1995)
Castaway Cowboy (Vincent McEveety, 1974)
Cinderella II: Dreams Come True (John Kafka, 2002)
Citizen Kane (Orson Welles, 1941)
Cocktail (Roger Donaldson, 1988)
Collateral (Michael Mann, 2004)
Colonel Heeza Liar in Africa (John Randolph Bray, 1913)
Color of Money, The (Martin Scorsese, 1986)
Comicolor Classics (Series: The Iwerks Studios, 1933–36)
Corpse Bride (Tim Burton and Mike Johnson, 2005)
Creature Comforts (Nick Park, 1989)
Death Becomes Her (Robert Zemeckis, 1992)
Debut of Thomas Cat, The (John Randolph Bray, 1920)
Destino (Dominique Monfery, 2003)
Dexter's Laboratory (Series: Cartoon Network Studios/Hanna-Barbera, 1996–2003)
Dirty Dali: A Private View (Guy Evans, 2007)
Disney–Pixar South Bank Show, The (Jonathan Levi, 2009)
Don Quixote (Ub Iwerks, 1934)
Drawn Together (Series: Comedy Central, 2004–2007)
Egyptian Melodies (Wilfred Jackson, 1931)
Enchanted Drawing, The (J. Stuart Blackton, 1900)
ET: The Extra-Terrestrial (Steven Spielberg, 1982)
Eyes in Outer Space (Ward Kimball, 1959)
Family Guy (Series: 20th Century Fox Television/Film Roman Productions/Fuzzy Door Productions/Hands Down Entertainment, 1999–to date)
Fantasmagorie (Émile Cohl, 1908)
Felix the Cat (Series: The Pat Sullivan Studio, 1919–30)

Final Fantasy VII: Advent Children (Tetsuya Nomura and Takeshi Nozue, 2005)
Final Fantasy: The Spirits Within (Hironobu Sakaguchi and Moto Sakakibara, 2001)
Finding Nemo (Andrew Stanton and Lee Unkrich, 2003)
For a Few Dollars More (Sergio Leone, 1965)
Forest Gump (Robert Zemeckis, 1994)
Gerald McBoing-Boing (Robert Cannon, 1951)
Gertie the Dinosaur (Winsor McCay, 1914)
Gone With the Wind (Victor Fleming, 1939)
Good Morning, Vietnam (Barry Levinson, 1987)
Good, The Bad, and The Ugly, The (Sergio Leone, 1966)
Grasshopper and the Ants, The (Wilfred Jackson, 1934)
Gulliver's Travels (Dave Fleischer, 1939)
Hannah Montana (Series: Disney Channel, 2006–to present)
Headless Horseman, The (Ub Iwerks, 1934)
Heaven's Gate (Michael Cimino, 1980)
Herbie Rides Again (Robert Stevenson, 1974)
High School Musical (Kenny Ortega, 2006)
Home Alone (Chris Columbus, 1990)
Humorous Phases of Funny Faces (J. Stuart Blackton, 1906)
Imperfect Lens, The (DVD Special Feature: *WALL-E*, 2008)
Incredibles, The (Brad Bird, 2004)
Iron Giant, The (Brad Bird, 1999)
Jaws (Steven Spielberg, 1975)
Jazz Singer, The (Alan Crosland, 1927)
Jumanji (Joe Johnston, 1995)
Jungle Book 2, The (Steve Trenbirth, 2003)
Jurassic Park (Steven Spielberg, 1993)
Kiki's Delivery Service (Hayao Miyazaki, 1989)
Kindergarten Cop (Ivan Reitman, 1990)
Land Before Time, The (Don Bluth, 1988)
Lil Swee' Pea (Dave Fleischer, 1936)
Look of Lilo and Stitch, The. (DVD Special Feature: *Lilo and Stitch*, 2002)
Look Who's Talking Too (Amy Heckerling, 1990)
Looney Tunes (Series: Leon Schlesinger Studios/Warner Bros. Pictures, 1930–69)
Magic Riddle, The (Yoram Gross, 1991)
Making of 'The Little Mermaid', The (Robert Heath, 1989)
Man and the Moon (Ward Kimball, 1955)
Man in Space (Ward Kimball, 1955)
Manhattan (Woody Allen, 1979)
Many Adventures Winnie the Pooh, The (John Lounsbery and Wolfgang Reitherman, 1977)
Mars and Beyond (Ward Kimball, 1957)
Mary Poppins (Robert Stevenson, 1964)
Mickey Mouse (Series: Walt Disney Productions, 1928–99)
Mickey Mouse Club (Series: Walt Disney Productions, 1955–1996)
Monsters, Inc. (Pete Docter, David Silverman and Lee Unkrich, 2001)

Mr. Bug Goes to Town (Dave Fleischer, 1941)
My Neighbor Totoro (Hayao Miyazaki, 1988)
My Old Kentucky Home (Max Fleischer, 1926)
Once Upon a Time in the West (Sergio Leone, 1968)
Oswald the Lucky Rabbit (Series: Robert Winkler Productions/Walter Lantz Productions, 1927–43)
Out of the Inkwell (Series: Inkwell Studios/Out of the Inkwell Films, 1919–29)
Pete's Dragon (Don Chaffey, 1977)
Porco Rosso (Hayao Miyazaki, 1992)
Princess and the Frog – The Return to Hand Drawn Animation, The (Unknown, 2009; Online Video Clip, accessed 15 September 2010: http://www.awntv.com/videos/the-princess-and-the-frog-featurette)
Princess Mononoke (Hayao Miyazaki, 1997)
Pulp Fiction (Quentin Tarantino, 1994)
Quest for Camelot (Frederik Du Chau, 1998)
Rabbit Rampage (Chuck Jones, 1955)
Ramona (Edwin Carewe, 1928)
Ratatouille (Brad Bird and Jan Pinkava, 2007)
Robin Hood: Prince of Thieves (Kevin Reynolds, 1991)
S1m0ne (Andrew Niccol, 2002)
Seventh Heaven (Frank Borzage, 1927)
Shanghai Noon (Tom Dey, 2000)
Shrek Forever After (Mike Mitchell, 2010)
Silly Symphonies (Series: Walt Disney Productions, 1929–39)
Simpsons, The (Series: 20th Century Fox Television/Gracie Films, 1989–to date)
Sinking of the Lusitania, The (Winsor McCay, 1918)
Skeleton Dance, The (Ub Iwerks and Walt Disney, 1929)
Song Car-Tunes (Series: Out of the Inkwell Films, 1924–27)
South Park (Series: Braniff Productions/Parker-Stone Studios, 1997–to date)
Spellbound (Alfred Hitchcock, 1945)
Splash (Ron Howard, 1984)
Stanley and Stella (Larry Malone, 1987)
Star Trek: The Motion Picture (Robert Wise, 1979)
Star Wars: Episode I – The Phantom Menace (George Lucas, 1999)
Star Wars: Episode IV – A New Hope (George Lucas, 1977)
Star Wars: Episode V – The Empire Strikes Back (Irvin Kershner, 1980)
Steamboat Willie (Walt Disney and Ub Iwerks, 1928)
Swan Princess, The (Richard Rich, 1994)
Talkartoons (Series: Fleischer Studios, 1929–32)
TateShot: Salvador Dalí and Walt Disney a Surreal Collaboration (Richard Stafford, 2007)
Terminator 2: Judgment Day (James Cameron, 1991)
Three Little Pigs (Burt Gillet, 1933)
Three Men and a Little Lady (Emile Ardolino, 1990)
Titan A.E. (Don Bluth, Gary Goldman and Art Vitello, 2000)
Toy Story (John Lasseter, 1995)
Toy Story 2 (John Lasseter, Ash Brannon and Lee Unkrich, 1999)

Toy Story 3 (Lee Unkrich, 2010)
Transformers Video Interview: Cast and Characters (Unknown, 2006; Online video clip, accessed 10 September 2010: http://www.youtube.com/watch?v=2cy8UbzQ6OA)
Transformers: The Movie (Nelson Shin, 1986)
Trolley Troubles (Walt Disney, 1927)
Tron (Steven Lisberger, 1982)
Tron: Legacy (Joseph Kosinski, 2010)
Truth About Mother Goose, The (Bill Justice and Wolfgang Reitherman, 1957)
Un Chien Andalou (Luis Buñel, 1929)
Up (Pete Doctor and Bob Peterson, 2009)
Wallace and Gromit in The Wrong Trousers (Nick Park, 1993)
WALL-E (Andrew Stanton, 2008)
What Price Glory (Raoul Wash, 1926)
Who Framed Roger Rabbit (Robert Zemeckis, 1988)
Who Killed Cock Robin (David Hand, 1935)
Winnie the Pooh and a Day for Eeyore (Rick Reinert, 1983)
Winnie the Pooh and the Blustery Day (Wolfgang Reitherman, 1968)
Winnie the Pooh and the Honey Tree (Wolfgang Reitherman, 1966)
Winnie the Pooh and Tigger Too (John Lounsbery, 1974)
Young Sherlock Holmes (Barry Levinson, 1985)

Index

Page numbers in **bold** denote figures. Where reference is made to an item that appears within a footnote this is denoted by the inclusion of a lowercase 'n' after the numeral.